Symbel
A Journal of Early Germanic Studies

Editorial Board
Stephen E. Flowers, Ph.D.: Germanic Religion and Runology
Stephen C. Wehmeyer, Ph.D.: Folklore
Glenn Alexander Magee, Ph.D.: Modern Philosophy
James A. Chisholm, D.J.: Legal History
Michael Moynihan: Graduate Student Representative

Acknowledgments
Special thanks go to Tom Wulf for his initial proofreading of the English translation of the Magnus Olsen article and to Michael Moynihan for his editorial work on the whole of the journal. Any errors are the full responsibility of the publisher.

Cover Art:
Shows image from Denmark IK 39 (X)-B Bracteate 450-550 CE. This bracteate contains runes and rune-like signs, and iconography perhaps relating to trifunctional symbolism with figures holding oath-ring, hammer and spear. Used with permission.

Lodestar Reissue

Published by
The Woodharrow Institute for Germanic and Runic Studies
Copyright © 2006

Symbel
A Journal of Early Germanic Studies

Number 1
(Fall 2006)

Articles

Presenting *Symbel* and the Woodharrow Institute for Germanic and Runic Studies		1
Elf-Quern and Elf-Shot: Language of Healing and Harming in Germanic Ritual Practice	Stephen C. Wehmeyer	3
On Magical Runes [1916]	Magnus Olsen	27
The Germanization of Christianity in the *Theologia Germanica*	Glenn Alexander Magee	49
The State of Traditional Germanic and Scandinavian Studies in the Universities of the United States	Michael Moynihan	69

Reviews

Brian Murdoch and Malcolm Read, eds. *Early Germanic Literature and Culture*. — 78

John McKinnell and Rudolf Simek with Klaus Düwel. *Runes, Magic and Religion: A Sourcebook*. — 78

Greg Mogenson. *Northern Gnosis: Thor, Baldr, and the Volsungs in the Thought of Freud and Jung*. — 80

Stephen E. Flowers. *The Northern Dawn*, Volume 1. — 81

Presenting *Symbel* and the Woodharrow Institute for Germanic and Runic Studies

The Woodharrow Institute was formed in the year 2002 by a small group of academics in a variety of disciplines who came to understand that the traditional study of ancient and medieval Germanic culture was being increasingly neglected in the established academic institutions. Our interest is in the preservation and promotion of early (pre-1500) Germanic studies, as well as the study of the survivals and revivals of cultural patterns stemming from this period. Chiefly our interests lie with *symbolic culture, myth, magic, folklore, history of religion, mysticism, runology and semiotics.*

Additionally, we support and promote interest in general Indo-European studies, especially as they serve as both a background to Germanic culture and as a basis for understanding neighboring Indo-European peoples who mutually influenced, and were influenced by, archaic Germanic culture.

Our aims are the promotion, preservation and restoration of early Germanic (pre-1500) and Indo-European studies.

Articles written for our official organ, *Symbel*, are peer reviewed by a panel of credentialed experts. Articles written for any of the Woodharrow publications should be of the highest academic standard, yet should be aimed at the college-educated non-specialist. We want to make our ideas intelligible across the disciplines, and strongly believe in an interdisciplinary approach, or even a synthetic or unified overarching discipline, in the study of early culture. Additionally, we strongly believe that our studies should be understood as meaningful and applicable to the intellectual and spiritual life of present-day individuals and cultures, not something which is a mere collection of moribund curiosities.

Membership in the WI is open to any and all who support our general aims, regardless of educational background. We are in dire need of an increased number of academics, active or retired, who share our aims. We encourage authors to write for our publications who have Ph.D. degrees or equivalent, those who are active teachers at any level of instruction, as well as distinguished students at all levels of education.

The Woodharrow Institute is in no way affiliated with any religious or political cause, group or faction. Our entire purpose is the promotion of traditional Germanic and Indo-European studies.

Elf-Quern and Elf-Shot
The Sensuous Language of Healing and Harming in Germanic Ritual Practice

Stephen C. Wehmeyer, Ph.D.

> [While] religion and magic share certain ritual features, the similarity is only formal. For instance the body in religious rituals is a public body: Participants enter states of embodiment that are meaningful in a communal sense above and beyond the simple sensory event. The bride becomes a wife by means of a religious ritual. Magical rituals, in contrast, are more likely to be private and intimate. Their power derives not from the social definition of a gesture but from the sensations and perceptions it evokes. ... While the religious ritual expresses public truths by means of the body, *the magical procedure is the grammar of sense experience.*
> Ariel Glucklich – *The End of Magic* (1997: 113-114) [emphasis mine]

Glucklich's exploration of the sensory dimensions of magic ritual practice in India is one example of an intriguing trend among those ethnographers, anthropologists and folklorists who study this most complex and subtle aspect of human behavior. In the last ten years or so, benchmark writings on magic and its practitioners have increasingly shifted our focus toward the role of the individual body and its senses as the tools by which, and the arena in which, meaning is made by magic. The most notable and innovative examples of what should perhaps be termed an *embodied* or *sensuous* approach to magic have largely emerged as the result of ethnographic studies of what are understood to be non-European cultures and modes of thinking (Sub-Saharan Africa, India, Sri Lanka, Haiti, Brazil, Venezuela, Afro-America). The articulation of this approach has thus far relied strongly on the researcher's ability to observe magical acts at first hand (often as an active participant), and to question specialists and their clients (and occasionally their victims!) directly about the sensory aspects of their experiences. This essay asks to what degree this embodied approach is applicable to European, and more specifically, Germanic magical practices,(1) specifically those which are not observed *in situ*, but rather known from historical documentation or from literary or mythological sources. Can we extract from the descriptions of early historians, mythographers, and antiquarians what Glucklich would call a "grammar of sense experience" for Germanic magic, and is such a thing a useful analytical tool? I would maintain that the *embodied* or *sensuous* approach is not only a viable, but in fact a *necessary* direction for the future study of Germanic magic, a point to which I will return in my concluding remarks. Furthermore, when analyzing the bodily elements in exemplary descriptions of magical ritual drawn from Saga literature, medieval *leechbooks*, and early collections of folk narrative, certain patterns emerge which suggest a coherent and distinctive sensuous "grammar" common to a diverse range of ritual acts. In the course of this examination, I wish to identify and analyze one of these patterns in particular: the *Oppositional Aesthetic Dyad*, which seems to be a central, pervasive, and characteristic element of Germanic magical ritual.(2)

I must acknowledge, before proceeding further, that I use the term "magic" rather freely throughout this essay, though it is a wildly contested and clearly problematic term from an historical and anthropological standpoint. Scholars like Karen L. Jolly have argued aggressively that several examples of ritual practice subsequently addressed in this essay (the Anglo-Saxon "Elf-Charms"), should in fact be considered to belong to the category of "popular religion," rather than "magic."(3) There is no question that the rituals I am analyzing herein often straddle generic categories, and might simultaneously be described as examples of "religious," "medical," or "magical" practice. As all are drawn from secondary or tertiary antiquarian sources or from medieval literature, rather than from ethnographic field research, we might also consider them to be examples of "supernatural belief" or "narratives *about* ritual" as much as they are rituals themselves. I do not believe, however, that these convoluted distinctions pose a very great problem for the inquiry at hand. While we may endlessly argue about the nature of the difference between magic and religion, or where one begins and the other ends, all of the rituals described below (whether actual, fictive, or a combination of the two) share commonalities which make it possible to analyze them comparatively. The specific structural similarities will be discussed in detail in subsequent pages. On the most basic level, however, I would maintain that all the rituals to be addressed here are, to paraphrase Jonathan Roper, patterned traditional behaviors, utterances, actions, postures, etc., "credited with the power to bring about changes in health, fortune, safety and emotional state." Such traditional forms are *"intended by their effect on supernature* to bring about change in the world in which we live."

(Roper 2003; italics mine). Given the comparable understanding of magic advanced by Wax and Wax (1962), Flowers (1986), Tambiah (1990), Glucklich (1997), etc. it is not at all inappropriate then to describe such rituals as "magic," though they may be other things as well. Each of these rituals supposes an ongoing interaction and *communication* with a subtle and largely hidden world that has the power to create change of a remarkable nature in the world of the seen and sensible. Paradoxically, it is through the portals of the senses, through the manipulation of physical sensory states, that the unseen world is accessed.

Sorcery and the Senses:

Some key examples of an embodied approach to magic

The idea that the sensory aspects of ritual, magical or otherwise, are important is not exactly a "new" concept in ritual scholarship. Much of the current trend can be considered and expansion of Claude Levi-Strauss' articulation of magic as a "science of the concrete," or as it is often glossed: "thinking in things." (Levi-Strauss 1966: chapter 2 *et passim*). In response to prior writers who asserted the "irrationality" of magic, Levi-Strauss maintained that magical thought is based upon an entirely rational and coherent system of classification by means of physical phenomena rather than abstract ideas. One should not, he reminds us, confuse logical sophistication with the tendency toward abstraction. Innumerable scholars have since taken up this tack, offering exegetical readings of religious and magical rites by correlating the physical symbols used in ritual with their ideological analogues, in order to determine what ritual symbols *mean* to those who employ them. In the midst of such structural analyses, however, scholars like Victor Turner have been forced to confront the fact that the sensory phenomena of ritual serve more than an analogical function:

> The symbols and their relations as found in *Isoma* are not only a set of cognitive classifications for ordering the Ndembu universe. They are also, and perhaps as importantly, a set of evocative devices for rousing, channeling, and domesticating powerful emotions, such as hate, fear, affection, and grief. They are also informed with purposiveness and have a "conative" aspect. In brief, *the whole person, not just the Ndembu "mind"* is existentially involved in the life or death issues with which Isoma is concerned (Turner 43; italics mine).

Well before the mind and its social persona absorbs and interprets the symbolic meanings of ritual elements, the body and its senses apprehend their aesthetic dimensions. The sensuous details of the magical act elicit responses from deep within the self without the filtering of conscious interpretation. The body's responses to the sensory stimuli in ritual form a subliminal baseline, against which the specific cultural "meanings" of the various symbols are laid down. The degree to which a ritual specialist, a practitioner of magic, can manipulate sensory stimuli to orchestrate somatic responses in herself, her clients, or victims, largely determines her skill as a sorcerer and the effectiveness of her practice.

In her ongoing work with a Haitian Vodou priestess and healer living in Brooklyn, New York, Karen McCarthy Brown has demonstrated the inextricability of the sensuous and the sorcerous. Vodou ritual, magic, and spirit possession all find their center in the sensory and sensual realities of the human body:

> Both understanding and remembering . . . can be seen as products of bodily labor. . . . Memory unaided by the five senses, and therefore by the fleshly body, is impoverished, shallow, and full of lacunae. Beyond remembering, the body can also explore, analyze and critique. We are, in and with our flesh, meaning-seekers and meaning-makers. (Brown 1995: 205)

In her essay "The Ritual Economy of Haitian Vodou" Brown explores how such meaning is sought and made through a series of deep sensory metaphors that form the core of Vodou cosmology and epistemology. "Within Vodou," she writes, "is a pervasive contrast between things that are bound or tied (*mare*) and things that have been loosed (*lage*), opened (*ouvri*), or made to flow (*koule*)." (Brown 1995: 220). Elsewhere she addresses the equally pervasive contrast between "hot" (*chofe*) and "cool" elements of Vodou ritual. In the close analysis of one ritual prescription designed to help a young woman negotiate a difficult personal relationship Brown demonstrates the skill of the ritual specialist at interlacing a series of powerful bodily experiences centered on binding and loosening, heating up and cooling down, all expressed through a host of sights, smells, sounds, and physical sensations which trigger profound emotional changes in her client. "Like a pool player, an accomplished healer knows how to slice into an emotional knot from exactly the right angle, so it will break into its constituent parts ... in a very real sense the healer's knowledge is carried in her body and it is addressed to the body of her client." (Brown 1995: 220) It is precisely this kind of focused somatic description and analysis that is lacking from so many ethnographic accounts of magical ritual. Brown demonstrates how much can be learned by addressing the sensory aspects of ritual *an sich*, by examining their concrete affective power at the individual level, before abstracting them to fit a broader social framework. This close reading of a single ritual moves us far closer to an understanding of how magic functions at the intimate, personal level—the level at which it is usually experienced.

Paul Stoller, who advocates an embodied or "sensuous" approach to anthropological or ethnographic writing in general, stresses the embodied nature of perception and cognition in "non-Western" societies:

> *Sensuous Scholarship* is an attempt to reawaken profoundly the scholar's body by demonstrating how the fusion of the intelligible and the sensible can be applied to scholarly practices and representations. In anthropology, for example, it is especially important to incorporate into ethnographic works the sensuous body, its smells, tastes, textures, and sensations. Such inclusion is especially paramount in the ethnographic description of societies in which the Eurocentric notion of text—and of textual interpretations—is not important. I have noted elsewhere why it is representationally and analytically important to consider how perception in non-Western societies devolves not simply from vision (and the linked metaphors of reading and writing) but also from smell, touch, taste and hearing. In many societies, these lower [sic] senses, all of which cry out for sensuous description, are central to the metaphoric organization of experience; they also trigger cultural memories (Stoller 1997: xv–xvi).

Stoller veers towards a kind of cultural essentialism with his suggestion that "disembodied" or "text-centered" thinking is necessarily Eurocentric or somehow a hallmark of putative "Western" culture, and by extension that "non-Western" cultures and individuals are somehow more viscerally perceptive. If his arguments are taken to their logical conclusion however, it becomes apparent that "sensuous scholarship" is as vital to the description and analysis of European religious and magical ritual as of ritual anywhere else in the world. Even the most superficial examination of European (specifically Germanic) magical practice reveals strong preoccupations with what Stoller terms the "lower senses," that is, "smell, touch, taste and hearing." While it is evident that the expressive works of European and American *academics* engaged in the study of magic often suffer from a lack of sensuousness, the traditions themselves are rich in somatic experiences, and are best understood from the perspective of an equally sensuous scholarship.

Ritual practice *in general* challenges the Cartesian ontological model that defines mind and body, body and world, as discrete and separate entities. The rituals described by Stoller, Brown, and Glucklich characterize systems of thought as (seemingly) divergent as Songhay sorcery, Haitian-American Vodou, and Indian Tantric healing. All are based upon a fundamental sense of the mutual interpenetration of the physical body and the world in which it lives. Ritual, regardless of cultural framework, establishes relationships between physical objects, words, or gestures; between interior states (like anger) and observable exterior phenomena (like a thunderstorm). Doing so it articulates the body as fundamentally *open* (via the senses) to seen and unseen worlds, which can enter it for good or ill. Despite Stoller's indictment of "Western" culture, one need only look at a few examples of Germanic magical belief and ritual practice to realize that they are strongly rooted in this non-Cartesian view of the body as an essentially *permeable* entity. Catharina Raudvere's analysis of shapeshifting beliefs and the pan-Scandinavian *mara* traditions, for example, demonstrates a widespread worldview in which the boundaries between self and other, thoughts and things, are permeable and fluid. Aggressive thoughts can take physical form, and a predatory spirit may be embodied in an everyday object like a pitchfork or a common farm animal. A cake of butter, flogged with a ritual whip, transfers its wounds to the physical body of a sorceress (Raudevere 1995: 48). In the specific examples of ritual to be subsequently discussed in this essay, we can likewise see the pervasiveness of this principle of bodily permeability. This material cries out for an appropriately "sensuous" analysis.

Moreover, Stoller insists that an essential part of adopting and applying a sensuous approach to scholarship involves the scholar: "lending his or her own body to the world." He asks us to cultivate an awareness of our sensory selves, so that sensuous experiences in the field can become tools for achieving a deeper understanding of particular cultural experiences as we document and analyze them. He likewise calls for the explicit description of the scholar's own bodily experiences, inviting us to become sensory participants in the worlds we describe, rather than distanced, disembodied eyes, recording and transmitting only the visual surface of an ethnographic experience.

Obviously, Stoller's proposed approach, together with those taken by scholars like Turner and Brown, seem far more applicable to the work of the ethnographer than to the historian, since the "sensuous experiences" of a scholar researching sixteenth-century Icelandic magic would consist almost entirely of the sounds, smells, and feelings of a university library! I believe, however, that a sensuous approach is both possible and needful for the analysis of historically documented magical practice. As in ethnography, it invites a shift in our attention, toward the raw, visceral experience of magic, as it can be teased out of textual descriptions or oral narratives. The involvement of the scholars body, in this case, demands a kind of active somatic imagination, in which we attempt to think about a given textual record with all of our senses, to find the meaning in the smells, tastes, sounds, and tactile sensations of a magical act, as much as in its visual components, or its socio-cultural niche. In a very real way this process enables us to "flesh out" textual descriptions of magical practice and gain a richer understanding of the impact these powerful acts were intended to have on the bodies of practitioners from the past.

While there are clear challenges to the kind of analysis I propose, lack of subject material is decidedly *not* one of them. Magical beliefs and practices are among the most prominent of folklore forms and examples collected by scholars of Germanic culture. The database of such things was rich and varied long before the formal articulation of Folklore as a discipline. Modern researchers have recourse to substantial collections of belief and practice compiled by such worthies as Afzelius (Sweden), Aarnasson (Iceland), Broman (Sweden), Grimm (pan-Germanic), et. al.; to say nothing of the evidence preserved in legal and ecclesiastical writings from the Medieval through the Early Modern periods, as well as material found in "primary" magical texts like the various Grimoires or *Galdrabækur* circulated from the 16th century onward.(4) Obviously any comprehensive analysis of Germanic magic would require several volumes, and be far beyond the scope of an interrogatory essay like this one. To illustrate the relevance of an embodied approach to this material, and offer a model for its continued application, I propose, instead, an analysis of a small sampling of closely related examples of magical ritual. Specifically, I wish to examine a selection of perceptions and practices that appeal to the simultaneously beneficial and dangerous qualities of the supernatural entities commonly known in Germanic folklore as *Elves*.

Personifying Permeability: Elves in Germanic Folk Belief

Elves, together with *huldrefolk*, mound people, trolls, *trows, skogsnurva*, and comparable supernatural beings, occupy a profoundly ambiguous position in Germanic folk belief and ritual practice, particularly from the Middle Ages onward. In mythological and saga literature we find them depicted as worthy of veneration, as recipients of sacrifice. The Eddic poem, *Lokasenna*, for example, depicts the Elves (ON *álfar*) together with the Æsir as part of the divine company drinking together in the house of Ægir:

Of vapn sín doma
oc vm vigrisni sina
sigtifa synir;
asa oc alfa,
er her inni ero,
mangi er þer i orði vinr.(5) [emphasis mine].

Citing *Olaf's Saga Helga*, Hilda Davidson likewise points out:

> [We] have evidence for their worship in Sweden during the early part of the eleventh century; Sigvat the Skald recorded his visit to a farm where *álfa-blót* was said to be in progress while on an errand for Olaf the Holy:

> Go thou in no further,
> Base wretch', the lady said;
> 'I fear the wrath of Othin,
> For we are heathen people.'
> That unattractive lady,
> Who drove me from her dwelling,
> Curtly, like a wolf, declared she
> Held elf-sacrifice within.' (Davidson 1943: 114).

It is important to note that such an *álfa-blót* is not likely to have been performed solely for altruistic devotional reasons. The idea of sacrifice as a means of achieving pragmatic aims is well attested in mythological and Saga literature, and it should come as no surprise that the Elves are offered sacrifice to achieve prosperity, success, and personal healing. Davidson also notes that:

> Such a belief is also found in the sagas, since in one passage in *Kormáks Saga* (XXII) a witch, Þórdís, directs a man who desires to be healed from a serious wound to go to: "a mound *(hóll)* not far from here, in which dwell elves; take the bull which Kormákr slew, amid redden the outside of the hill with bull's blood, and make the elves a feast with the flesh; and you will he healed." (Davidson 1943: 111).

The trope of sacrificing to the Elves at a hill, mound, or sacred stone is quite important to this discussion, as it persists in various parts of the Germanic speaking world in the practice of making offerings at stones marked with what archeologists have come to call "cup and ring" motifs. These neolithic monuments are termed "Elf-mills" or "Elf-pots" (alf-qvarn) in Sweden, and "Elf-cups" elsewhere.

Neither is the less positive moral nature of the Elves absent from Saga literature, however, as we see in King Hrolf Kraki's Saga, where they league against Hrolf as part of the supernatural army assembled by the half-Elven witch, Skuld: "[She], to overpower her brother Hrolf, fashioned a spell of high potency, which summoned elves, norns, and countless other vile creatures. No human power could withstand such a force." (Byock, tr. 1998: 71)

Similarly, oral narratives and folk-medical traditions from the medieval period onward establish the Elves as capable of visiting misfortune on communities or individuals, and causing physical harm to humans or livestock. The belief is widespread throughout northern and western Europe as well as key regions of North America[6] that when angered, ignored, or simply out of their own mischievous nature, Elves are capable of firing invisible missiles which strike livestock or humans, causing debilitating or potentially fatal illness. The afflicted are said to be "Elf-Shot." Moreover, folklorist Lauri Honko (1959) posits Elf-Shot as belonging to a belief complex he terms *krankheitsprojektile*, "missile of disease/illness." This idea that disease or disorder results from the penetration of the physical body by a foreign object or substance (usually aimed by another with malicious intent) assumes and relies upon *a conception of the human body/self as a fundamentally penetrable entity*.

Furthermore, the basic ontological relationship of Elves to the human community is equally ambiguous, as they are mythologically depicted as divine or semi-divine beings who dwell (with the Æsir), while at the same time, Saga literature suggests that human dead who have been buried in mounds with the proper ceremony are sometimes accorded new names ending in the suffix "alfr."(7) In this form they receive ancestral veneration, which suggests that one archaic conception of the Elves identifies them with the deified dead (see Davidson 1943: chapter 4). Like the Dead, the Elves are capable of dispensing blessings or blights, and human interaction with them is a delicate affair. The mutual association of Elves and the Dead with *mounds*, or with the cup-marked stones mentioned previously, further strengthens their connection to the principle of permeability. The mound is a locus of interpenetration, where the underworld rises up to meet and be enveloped by this middle world, just as a shaft-grave, pit, well, or other deep hole constitutes a penetration of the underworld by this one. The cup-marked stones, protruding boulders marked with depressions, manage to be both at once. I will discuss the significance of these stones in detail subsequently, but for now I wish only to point out that as simultaneously penetrated and penetrating, the cup stones are dramatic zones of mutual permeability, liminal spaces par excellence. Their very topological nature marks them as places belonging to the Elves.

Given this widespread perception of a host of (mostly) unseen and entirely morally ambivalent forces co-existing with and interpenetrating the visible, tangible human world, it is hardly surprising that the Elves should be the focus of a substantial number of rituals throughout the Germanic world. Such rituals range from rites which appeal to the Elves for healing, to those which address illnesses caused by the Elves themselves, to those which seem designed to aim the destructive power of the Elves against an distant enemy. In each of these cases, a sensuous reading of the ritual as described reveals a consistent and repeated series of definitive visceral experiences, a common "language" of sensory stimuli. I would argue that the ritual orchestration of these specific sense experiences constitutes a coherent "grammar of sense perception" (to use Glucklich's term), which forms the basis of "Elf magic." This grammar is notably persistent through time and across space, and may well be one vital root of a pan-Germanic ritual structure.

The Elf-Mill:
Sensuous Structure and the Oppositional Aesthetic Dyad

> There are still to be found elf-altars, where offerings are made for the sick. The so-called wise women—the Horgabrudar of our days—anoint with swine's fat, which was used in the pagan offerings, and read prayers, which they say are mystic; after which something metallic, that has been worn or borne by the sick person—a small coin or even a pin is sufficient—and lastly a cross (as a token that the Savior's power is also here superstitiously invoked) are laid upon the elf-mill (*älf-qvarn*) or, as it is also called, elf-pot (*älf-gryta*). These conjuring women (*signerskor*), when they are called to the sick, usually begin with pouring melted lead into water, and judge that the disease has been caused by Elves; when having secured payment, they commence a new juggle, which they call "striking down," or "anointing for the Elves," at sunset on the following Thursday. Some country people will anoint the elf-mill without applying to a cunning woman; These read no prayers but only sigh out: "Lord, help me!" (Thorpe 2001: 272).

In contrast to the complex rituals documented at first hand by latter day ethnographers of magic, this might seem a hopelessly scanty and problematic passage with which to begin. This is Benjamin Thorpe's sanitized, bowdlerized, mid-Victorian paraphrase of a description drawn from Afzelius' *Svenska Folkets Sago-Hafder* (1844), itself an antiquarian text considerably abstracted from any actual performance of this ritual. Nevertheless, I would argue that even in such an attenuated description, there is much to be learned from a sensuous reading of the ritual as we have it here.

In order to understand the way in which sensory stimuli are organized in the performance of this ritual, I wish to introduce a concept I have chosen to call the *Oppositional Aesthetic Dyad*. I use this term to describe a single ritual act or behavior in which two opposite or alternative sensory stimuli are directly juxtaposed. The Oppositional Aesthetic Dyad (hereafter "OAD") proves to be an elemental and strongly persistent "niche" in Germanic ritual structure. We might call it, after Propp, a ritual *allomotif*, into which a wide array of possible aesthetic motifemes might be slotted in an individual ritual. Such paired stimuli can include elements that are olfactory (acrid/fragrant, fresh/fermented), visual (bright/dull, visible/hidden), aural (audible/silent, loud/soft, harmonious/discordant), gustatory (bitter/sweet) or somatic (hard/soft, rigid/malleable, hot/cold, dry/wet, rough/smooth).

The presence of dyadic structure in ritual is a well-attested fact of anthropology. Levi-Strauss (1966), Turner (1969), and innumerable others have clearly demonstrated the importance of binary juxtaposition or dialectics in ritual structure. As suggested previously, however, past analyses have focused primarily on the symbolic and referential nature of such binary elements: their correlation to abstract social concepts, their ability to "stand for" something other than they are. I, on the other hand, choose to root my descriptions and analyses very strongly in the affective properties of the aesthetic dyad, rather than on its representative correlation to social realities or philosophical categories.

Although the symbolic meaning ascribed to any pair of sensory stimuli is of course vital to an understanding of their role in ritual, what marks a given dyad as specifically "magical" in my terminology is its ability to affect at the visceral, sensuous level. It is for this very reason that we find identical dyadic pairs as the building blocks of magical rites from diverse cultures, whose people may ascribe very different symbolic referents to the same sensory experiences. The sensory language of the magician often transcends individual culture. Of course, since magical ritual is often undertaken to effect change in the social sphere, the particular social meaning of a given ritual symbol must be taken into account, but only *after* its aesthetic qualities have been sufficiently addressed.

I believe these oppositional dyads function as they do in ritual by causing the body of the practitioner, as well as those of any other participants including the patient or victim (if present) to oscillate between dramatically opposing sense experiences, creating a strong perceptual atmosphere of *change*. An ingrained sense of inherent dynamism of experience and a resultant belief in the capacity of change is of course essential to the idea of magic, focused as it is on causing observable change of one sort or another in the objective world. The orchestration of aesthetic tensions through the manipulation of a number of these dyads creates a frisson pregnant with possibility as the physical senses of the practitioner, patient, or victim shift to accommodate differing sensations, thus communicating on a deep, non-verbal level that radical, dramatic change is not merely possible, but inevitable.

If we attempt a sensuous reading of the Elf-Quern ritual described above, we can clearly see how a series of oppositional aesthetic dyads are arranged to create the atmosphere conducive to a change in health. According to Thorpe's account, the ritual begins with a diagnostic divination by molybdomancy, the widespread traditional practice of pouring molten lead in water and interpreting the resulting shapes, to determine the origin of the sick person's illness. In this case, the technique is used to determine whether or not the affliction has been caused by Elves, to which the healer can then appeal for the patient's relief. Most (non-sensuous) analyses would focus on the interpretive process by which the diviner/healer ascribes meaning to the shapes assumed by the molten lead, but I would maintain that quite apart from this mantic interpretation, the experience is effective on a non-verbal, non-semiotic, physiological level, as even this initial procedure is rife with pure aesthetic opposition. The practice involves dyadic experiences of solid/liquid (cold lead/molten lead) heat/cold (molten lead/cold water), malleable/rigid (molten lead/cooled lead). This rapid oscillation between opposite sensory stimuli is powerful in its own right, and introduces the atmosphere of dynamism and malleability in which the ritual Thorpe calls "striking down" is to take place. It is highly significant that this rite should center on the cup stones, here called "Elf-Pots" or "Elf-Querns." As suggested previously, the cup markings on prominent stones offer the aesthetic juxtaposition of "protrusion/depression" or perhaps more accurately: "concave/convex." The stones themselves are constantly in a state of aesthetic tension. Out of this tension, which as we see can be further enhanced by the ritualistic application of a host of other comparable sensory dyads, emerges the stones' capacity to serve as zones and markers of a specific kind of spiritual power within an appropriate cultural framework.

We can see many of the same aesthetic dyads employed throughout the remainder of this rite. Thorpe tells us that the elf-quern is anointed "with swine's fat," which practice involves several sensory juxtapositions: hard/soft or rigid/malleable (hard rock/soft fat), cold/warm, dry/wet, and dull/shining (as the application of fat would make the rock glisten)(8). The metallic object laid upon the altar (a coin or pin) further enhances this latter juxtaposition, as what was at the outset a sheenless stone is now made replete with shining elements.(9) Although Thorpe himself advances a predictably antiquarian analysis of the swine's fat, "which was used in pagan offerings," as deriving from pre-Christian sacrificial practices, we should consider the common aesthetic strategies at the root of both the "original" pagan rites and this later syncretic practice. The comparable healing rite described in Kormak's Saga (cited previously), requires that the wounded hero "redden" the mound with the bull's blood, a procedure that employs precisely the same sensory juxtapositions described above. Furthermore, in the Eddic poem "Hyndlulijoð," the goddess Freyja speaks of the piety of her devoted hero, Ottar, saying:

> Haurg hann mer gerdi hladinn steinum
> — nu er griot þat
> at gleri vordit —,
> raud hann i nyiu
> nauta blodi,
> æ trvdi Ottar
> a asyniur.

The poet, speaking for the goddess, foregrounds the aesthetic juxtaposition, dull/shining as the sacred act which in effect compels Freyja's divine response to Ottar's need. Freyja grants Ottar's desire *not* because she is touched by his piety, honored or well fed by his sacrifice, but *"hladinn steinum nu er griot þat at gleri vordit"*: because "he has made the [dull] rocks [of her *horgr*] shine."

Thorpe concludes his gloss of the Elf-Quern rite by pointing out that ordinary folk who are not ritual specialists may also anoint the Elf-Mill, "These read no prayers, but only sigh out "Lord, help me!" While I will not be so reductive as to suggest that any incantatory aspects of this rite are unimportant, this bit of information does suggest the fundamental affective power of the ritual's somatic elements.

The celebrated "Elf-Charms" of late Anglo-Saxon *leechcraft* have been the subject of exhaustive analysis by folklorists and scholars of religion and ethno-medicine [Grendon (1909) Storms (1948), Grattan and Singer (1952), Cameron (1993), Jolly (1996)]. Like the Swedish Elf-Quern rite, these charms are intended to heal ailments caused by the supernatural missiles of Elves or other invisible agents. The most notable recent work in this vein, Jolly's *Popular Religion in Late Saxon England*, addresses the interplay and juxtaposition of Pagan and Christian themes and structures in the charms.(10) A close, sensuous reading of the same charms reveals persistent and prominent instances of oppositional aesthetic juxtaposition as well. Two notable examples seem to be composed of interlacing oppositional aesthetic dyads. From *Lacnunga* CLXIV (97):

> Again for that [*aelfadle*—"elf disease"]. Lay under the altar these herbs, let nine masses be sung over them: incense, holy salt, three heads of cropleek, aelfthone's lower part, and helenium. Take in the morning a cup full of milk; drip thrice some holy water in it. Let him sip it as hot as he can. Eat with it three bits of aelfthone. When he wants to rest, have coals there inside. Lay incense and aelfthone on the coals, and smoke him with that until he sweats; and smoke the house throughout; and eagerly sign the man. And when he goes to rest, let him eat three bits of helenium, and three of cropleek, and three of salt. And let him have a cup full of ale and drip thrice holy water in it. Let him eat each bit; then let him rest. Do this for nine mornings and nine nights. It will soon be well with him. (Jolly 1996: 161-2).

The procedure here involves ingesting a series of herbs and liquids at morning and evening together with a rigorous application of heat and herbal smoke to promote sweating. Apart from the employment of the mass, holy water, and the sign of the cross, this "charm" seems relatively free of ritualistic behavior, and thus not necessarily appropriate for the structural analysis I propose. I maintain, however, that the non-Christian elements of the charm consist in fact, of a carefully orchestrated series of OADs, and that a deep ritual structure lies at the heart of what would otherwise seem to be merely a prescription for a course of medicinal preparations. To begin with, two healing drinks with accompanying herbs are administered, alternately at morning and evening. In the morning, a hot cup of milk, together with aelfthone, and at evening, ale with helenium, cropleek, and salt. The dyadic structure begins to look like this:

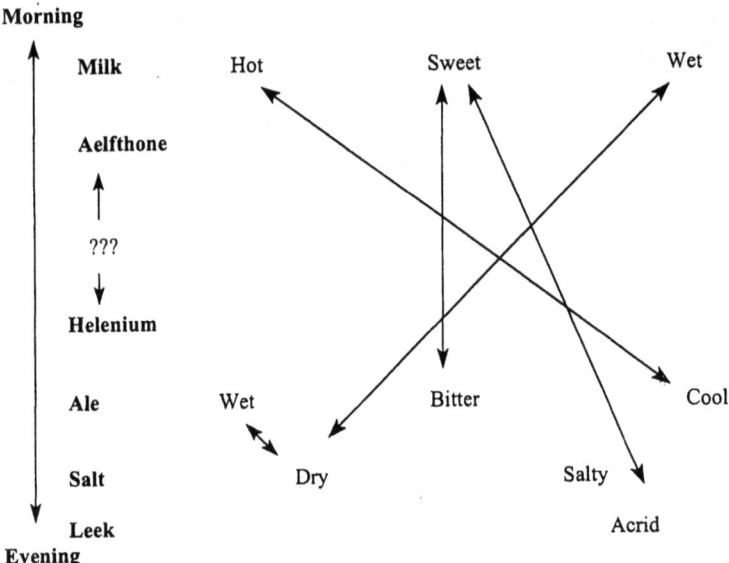

The difficulty in accurately classifying either Aelfthone or Helenium (See Grattan and Singer 1952, Jolly 1996) makes it impossible to reliably assign aesthetic qualities to these two herbs, but I suspect that if we were able to determine their relative tastes, smells, or appearances, each would aesthetically oppose the other and/or other aesthetic elements in the rite. The application of smoke to induce sweating adds further aesthetic tension to this ritual, thus:

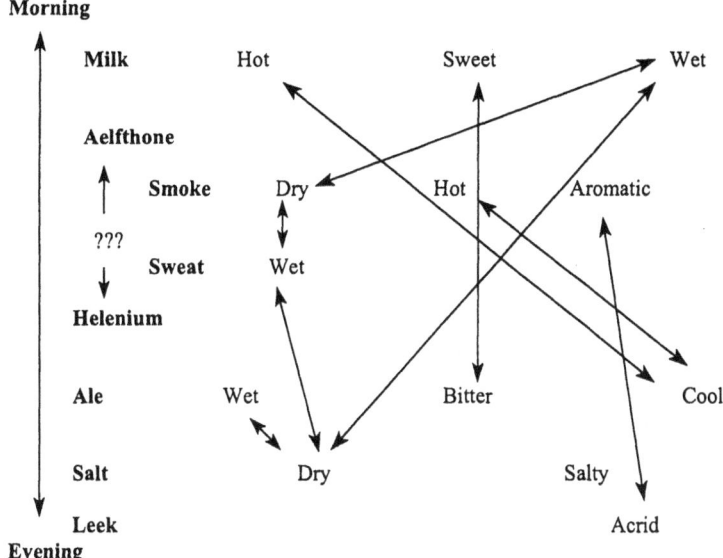

I think the influence of the OAD as a dominant structural element in this particular example is now clearly evident.

As this charm comes to us from a medieval *medical* manual, we must take into consideration the very definite possibility that the principles of aesthetic opposition here derive from the highly influential Greek medical theory of the four humors (with their attendant sensory qualities) rather than from a more expressly Germanic source. I would, in turn, argue that while this is certainly possible, the persistence of the OAD in the structure of rites not so obviously influenced by Mediterranean textual traditions of medicine and healing suggests that this particular example represents the confluence of two parallel, complimentary streams of thought. The theory of the four bodily humours would no doubt find the Germanic imagination fertile ground in which to take root, as the latter is predisposed to think in terms of dynamic aesthetic oppositional structure.

Another Anglo-Saxon example of a charm for Elf-Shot which bears mention is found in *Lacnunga* CXXXIV-CXXXV (75–76), and glossed as a prescription *"wið færstice"* [for a sudden stitch]. It consists of a lengthy incantation to be recited while a selection of herbs is boiled in butter (conceivably to be ultimately used as a salve or other topical medicine). "Feverfew," it begins, "and the red nettle that grows into a house [or "in the grain"] and waybroad; boil in butter..." (tr. Jolly 1996: 139). After the incantation (which we will examine subsequently), a knife is plunged into the hot herbal preparation. Jolly suggests that thus prepared, the knife might be used to lance the afflicted area, although this is not prescribed in the charm text itself.

For our purposes, if we consider these actions *an sich*, they frame the incantation with several clear OAD's. The herbs themselves have oppositional aesthetic qualities: Nettle is "sharp" to the touch and astringent when eaten or drunk, and waybroad (plantain), is broad, soft, and fleshy in comparison. The herbs are then are boiled in butter (soft, hot, malleable) into which is plunged a knife (hard, cold, rigid). Whatever else is going on, the ritual actions of the charm employ the same dyadic structure (and many of the same specific sensuous elements) which we find in the rituals discussed previously. The incantation proper offers an intriguing example of the way in which this structure translates onto the verbal level, as it makes reference to a number of sensory dyads, in addition to those expressed in the non-verbal portion of the charm. The text runs as follows:

> Loud were they, lo loud,   when they rode over the mound,
> they were fierce   when they rode over the land.
> Shield yourself now   that you may escape this evil.
> Out, little spear,   if herein you be!
> Stood under linden,   under a light shield,
> where the mighty women   readied their power,
> and they screaming   spears sent.
> I back to them   again will send another,
> a flying dart   against them in return.
> Out, little spear,   if herein it be!
> Sat a smith,   forged he a knife,
> little iron   strong wound.
> Out, little spear,   if herein it be!
> Six smiths sat,   war-spears they made.
> Out, spear,   not in, spear!
> If herein be   a bit of iron,
> hag's [*haegtesse*] work,   it shall melt.
> If you were in the skin shot,   or were in flesh shot,
> or were in the blood shot,   or were in bone shot,
> or were in limb shot,   may your life never be torn apart.
> If it were Aesir shot,   or it were elves' shot,
> or it were hag's shot,   now I will help you.
> This your remedy for Aesir shot,   this your remedy for Elves' shot;
> This your remedy for hag's shot; I will help you.
> It fled there into the mountains. . . . no rest had it.
> Whole be you now!   Lord help you!(11) (Jolly 1996:139)

As the charm is intended to remove or destroy the invisible elf-missile (Honko's *krankheitsprojektile*) that has caused the stitch, the incantation repeats four times the phrase (with some variation) "**Out,** little spear if here**in** you be." Out and In are the fundamental dyadic pair addressed in this charm which aims to drive out an illness which has lodged itself inside the body. Phrases such as "If herein be a bit of **iron** .... it shall **melt**," further invoke the now familiar pairing of hard/soft or solid/liquid that seems common to each of these healing rites.

A still more subtle evocation of the same aesthetic pairings is found in the couplet: "If you were in the **skin** shot, / or were in **flesh** shot / or were in the **blood** shot / or were in **bone** shot," where skin (outside) is paired with flesh (inside), blood (liquid) with bone (solid). While the primary focus of this essay is the non-verbal grammar of magic, which speaks directly to the physical senses, an example like this one demonstrates the persistence of this structure in more specifically verbal forms.(12)

Thus far, we have explored the relevance of the OAD as an analytical construct for understanding rituals of *healing*. It would follow that such an elemental structural unit, if it is indeed as pervasive and fundamental as I maintain it to be, that it would be an essential part of the structure of the other face of healing: rituals of aggression, malice, and harm. As common as is the belief in "magic shot" (whether caused by elves, witches, sorcerers, or other malicious beings), we find few well articulated examples of rituals to aim and direct such missiles of disorder (or to impel beings like the elves to fire them). One notable exception is a very explicit description found in the writings of Olof Johan Broman, vicar at Hudicksvall in Sweden during the early part of the eighteenth-century. Broman's *Glysisvallur* is a multi-volume compendium of folk belief, custom, vernacular medicine, and genealogy. The work contains an extended discussion of Elf-shots, Finn-shots, and so forth, including Broman's account of the time he himself suffered such an attack at the hands of an angry sorcerer. After describing in detail the symptoms and effects of various types of *krankheitsprojektile*, Broman goes on to tell the reader exactly how such magic-shot is made:

> For it is a small ring made of an entwined soft twig taken from a certain kind of tree. This ring is placed on a stone which is stuck in the ground, and inside this ring one spits three times. Then a glowing coal is placed on it, and some charms are recited. Then another stone or axehead is taken, and with one powerful blow the ring is smashed asunder, and a crack is heard. This shot can be aimed at both man and beast, and often hits its mark. But others can be caught by the same shot, even though the employed marksman was not aiming at them. (Broman 1811, cited in Edsman 1961: 130).

There is no question that we have here an application of the same "grammar of sense experience" found in the previously cited examples of healing rites. Here, though employed for opposite ends, we again note the structural prominence of the OAD: A straight twig is bent into a ring (straight/curved), placed on a stone stuck in the ground (soft/hard). The sorcerer spits inside it (wet/dry), and a burning coal is placed on top (hot/cold—dry/wet). The final blow with (cold) stone or axehead completes the last dyad of (cold/hot). A vertical schematic illustrates how tightly these aesthetic dyads are interlaced, maximizing the opposition between them and heightening the tension of the ritual:

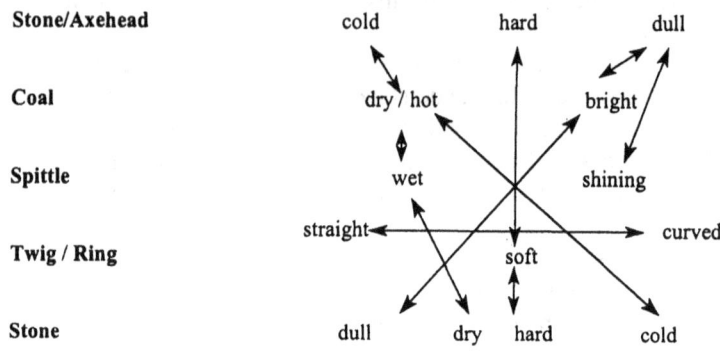

Out of this intense orchestration of aesthetic tension, the sorcerer's anger and hate take powerful, physical form. The body is played like a musical instrument, cycling through repeated themes of friction and conflict, building in pitch and energy, until the resounding *crack!* that ends the rite and sends the magic shot against the hapless victim. Ritual scholarship of past decades would make little, if anything, of what seems to be a simple enacting of aggressive feelings. But a sensuous reading, in which the scholar engages his or her own body to understand, reveals this rite for what it is: a message encoded in a sophisticated sensuous language, a rich vocabulary of the senses, structurally based upon the OAD which persists through time and across space as a strong traditional element in the Germanic magical and religious imagination.

In conclusion, I wish to return to the questions posed in my introductory remarks. Can a useful analytical tool be extracted by "sensuous" means from antique collections of folk-belief that can help us to better understand and appreciate the coherence and sophistication of Germanic ritual practice? And does "sensuous scholarship" as a directive have something to offer the study of Germanic magical traditions, particularly those of bygone eras? I think that this admittedly limited and preliminary inquiry indicates that we can indeed answer "yes" to both questions.

The OAD as a structural unit provides a relatively new and useful tool for describing Germanic magic and ritual, while pointing toward numerous avenues for further investigation and fruitful research. It clearly supports (and is supported by) the intuitive speculations of contemporary Norse scholars like Stephen Mitchell, who posits a polydyadic ritual assemblage as the basis for the various cryptic "Thistil-Mistil-Kistil" runic inscriptions that are venerated as powerful magic (Mitchell 1988: 30).(13) Is the OAD as constant and pervasive an element as my analysis here suggests? We cannot know until it is tested further against the rich and diverse corpus of Germanic belief, past and present. Exceptions will doubtless be found, but so will further supporting evidence.

The ritual arts of the Germanic speaking world developed as a result of centuries of intense thinking about, and skillfully working with, the body and its senses as a means of galvanizing change in the individual, the community, and the world. Sensuous scholarship offers us a chance to gain a more intimate understanding of just how developed and elaborate were these means for orchestrating the senses towards a focused end. As I have described it here, the trend toward sensuousness in scholarship emerges largely from the study of non-European peoples and cultures. Germanic studies, particularly where concerned with vernacular religion, ritual, folk medicine, or magic, cannot afford to be absent from this dialogue. Indeed, we have a mandate to become actively engaged in it: to learn from it and contribute our own voices to its discourse. Nor should ethnologists be loath to admit the validity of the sensuous approach to European culture, however much we are predisposed to romanticize and fetishize non-European bodies and the "Ethnographic Other." When scholars are willing to engage their senses in an imaginative way, when we remember the body as we think and write about people from whom we may be separated by thousands of miles or thousands of years, the flesh becomes an invaluable medium through which to see, hear, taste, touch, smell—thus better to know—the worlds of the past.

NOTES

(1) One might argue that any European magical practice which incorporates Judeo-Christian elements is in fact a hybrid or syncretic practice, with obvious roots in Middle-Eastern modes of thought, however often scholars are inclined to identify Christianity with "Western" thought and culture.

(2) I am actually inclined to consider the Oppositional Aesthetic Dyad as a universal characteristic of magic, regardless of cultural or temporal origin. However, for the purposes of this essay, I am content to suggest its pervasiveness in the ritual practices of cultures which may be called Germanic. Further research is necessary to determine its application outside these parameters, although my own ethnographic experience suggests that it has much more diverse application as an analytical construct.

(3) Jolly's articulation of popular religion is somewhat ponderous, and could benefit considerably from the integration of Leonard Primiano's alternative trope of *Vernacular Religion* which more elegantly reflects the complexities of religion as it is lived, in contrast to the idealized forms of religion often reified as "official." (see Primiano 1995).

(4) A substantial number of such works are currently archived and on display at the National Library in Reykjavik and in facsimiles at the Museum of Icelandic Sorcery and Witchcraft in Strandir. Selected translations of some famous "Black Books" have been published for the English speaking world: f. ex. *The Galdrabók*, (S. Flowers: Rûna-Raven, 2005, 2nd ed.), and *The Black Books of Elverum* (M. Rustad: Galde Press: 1999).

(5) All Eddic quotes are from the Bugge emendation c. 1867 unless otherwise indicated.

(6) See, for example, Barbara Reiti's "'The Blast' in Newfoundland Fairy Tradition," in Narváez 1991.

(7) One notable example is the case of King Olaf, brother of Halfdan, who after his death was given offerings in time of need and called "Geirstaðaálfr."

(8) The most exhaustive and comprehensive treatment of the wet/dry dyad as the foundation of apotropaic and health-related magic or luck beliefs is Alan Dundes's landmark study, "Wet and Dry, the Evil Eye: An Essay in Semitic and Indo-European Worldview" which appears in Newall's *Folklore Studies in the Twentieth Century* (see bibliography). To my knowledge no more thorough exposition of the power and prominence of a single dyad exists.

(9) It is perhaps significant that the Swedish *alf*, Old Norse *álfar* and O.E. *elf*, *ælf*, all derive from P.Gmc. *albiz*, origin unknown, possibly from PIE *albho-* "white" or *"shining."*

(10) Jolly primarily concentrates on a textual analysis of the charms' verbal components (although she does discuss the syncretic aspects of some of the non-verbal, ritual procedures used in the charms).

(11) This last adjuration to the deity recalls the detail from Thorpe's elf-quern rite which can be conducted by those who anoint and sigh out "Lord help me!"

(12) Still another, very straightforward example is the common English charm against burns (sometimes erysipelas) cataloged by Jonathan Roper (2003) among others, one version of which runs:

There were two giants came from the East,
*One wrought **fire** and the other wrought **frost**;*
***Out fire** and **in frost**;*
In the name of Father, Son and Holy Ghost.

(Recorded in Devon, also cited in Porter 1905: 108)

(13) Regarding the "Thistil-Mistil-Kistill" cryptogram, Mitchell (1988: 30) writes:

"It is probable that the first two elements of this trilogy refer to the 'widespread magic herbs' (*vidtutbredte trylleurtur*) mistletoe and thistle, perhaps even these two gathered and preserved in the third item, a small chest. It is a tempting image, indeed, with the *pistill-mistil(tein)* dyad projecting simultaneously the complexities of life and death, reversed barrenness and fertility, nestled side-by-side in a little chest (*kistill*). In the case of mistletoe (*Viscum Album*), one sees the image of life-in-death, a regardless-of-season evergreen plant, its cut-and-dried shape as verdant and lifelike as it was on the tree ... in the other instance, one imagines the brittle, dry, brown husk of the thistle ... yet contained within that dead, withered and seemingly useless head surrounded by prickly bracts, are the seeds from which will spring dozens, perhaps hundreds of new plants."

Whether we accept the interpretive gloss of "life-in-death" or "death-in-life," this purported sacred assemblage contains enough OADs to merit a structural analysis all its own.

Bibliography

Brown, Karen McCarthy. 1991. *Mama Lola.* Berkeley: University of California Press.

———. 1995. "Serving the Spirits: The Ritual Economy of Haitian Vodou" in Donald J. Cosentino, ed. *Sacred Arts of Haitian Vodou.* Los Angeles: Fowler Museum of Cultural History. pp. 205–223.

Byock, Jesse. 1988. *The Saga of King Hrolf Kraki.* London: Penguin.

Cosentino, Donald J, ed. 1995. *Sacred Arts of Haitian Vodou.* Los Angeles: Fowler Museum of Cultural History.

Dundes, Alan. 1980. "Wet and Dry, the Evil Eye: An Essay in Semitic and Indo-European Worldview" in Venetia J. Newall, ed. *Folklore Studies in the Twentieth Century.* Totowa, New Jersey: Rowman & Littlefield. Pp. 37–63.

Edsman, Carl-Martin. 1967. *A Swedish Female Folk Healer from the Beginning of the 18th Century.* Uppsala: Almqvist & Wiskells Boktrykeri AB.

Ellis, Hilda Roderick. 1943. *The Road to Hel.* Cambridge: Cambridge University Press.

Flowers, Stephen E. 1986. *Runes and Magic: magical formulaic elements in the older runic tradition.* (American University Studies. Series I, Germanic Languages and Literatures, vol. 53). New York: Peter Lang.

Grattan, J. H. C. and Charles Singer. 1952. *Anglo-Saxon Magic and Medicine.* Publications of the Wellcome Historical Medical Museum. Oxford: Oxford University Press.

Georges, Robert A. and Michael Owen Jones. 1995. *Folkloristics: An Introduction.* Bloomington: Indiana University Press.

Glucklich, Ariel. 1997. *The End of Magic.* New York: Oxford University Press.

Honko, Lauri. 1959: *Krankheitsprojektile.* Helsinki (FF Communications 178).

Jolly, Karen Louise. 1996. *Popular Religion in Late Saxon England: Elf Charms in Context.* Chapel Hill and London: University of North Carolina Press.

Kvideland Reimund and Henning Sehmsdorf, eds. 1988. *Scandinavian Folk Belief and Legend.* Minneapolis: University of Minnesota Press.

Levi-Strauss, Claude. 1966. *The Savage Mind.* Chicago: University of Chicago Press.

Mitchell, Stephen A. 1988. "Anaphrodesiac Charms in the Nordic Middle Ages: Impotence, Infertility, and Magic" in *Norveg: Journal of Norwegian Folk Studies,* vol. 41, no. 1: 19–42.

Morgan, David. 1998. *Visual Piety – a History and Theory of Popular Religious Images.* Berkeley/Los Angeles: University of California Press.

Narváez, Peter 1991. "Newfoundland Berry Pickers 'In the Fairies': Maintaining Spacial, Temporal, and Moral Boundaries through Legendry" in Peter Narváez, ed. *The Good People: New Fairylore Essays.* Lexington: University Press of Kentucky.

Obeyesekere, Gananath. 1981. *Medusa's Hair: An Essay on Personal Symbols and Religious Experience.* Chicago: University of Chicago Press.

Primiano, Leonard. 1995. "Vernacular Religion," in *Western Folklore* 54, no. 1: 37–56.

Raudvere, Catherina. 1995. "Analogy Narratives and Fictive Rituals: Some Legends of the *Mara* in Scandinavian Folk Belief" in *ARV: Nordic Yearbook of Folklore,* vol. 4: 41–62.

Reiti, Barbara.1991. "The Blast in Newfoundland Fairy Tradition" in Peter Narváez, ed. *The Good People: New Fairylore Essays.* Lexington: University Press of Kentucky.

Roper, Jonathan. 2003. "Towards a Poetics, Rhetorics, and Proxemics of Verbal Charms" in *Folklore: An Electronic Journal of Folklore* (www.folklore.ee/folklore): (Folk Belief and Media Group of the Estonian Literary Museum), vol. 24.

Sklar, Deidre. 1994. "Can Bodylore Be Brought to Its Senses?" *Journal of American Folklore,* vol. 107, no. 423: 9–22.

Stallybrass, Peter and Allon White. 1986. *The Poetics and Politics of Transgression.* Ithaca: Cornell University Press.

Stoller, Paul. 1997. *Sensuous Scholarship.* Philadelphia: University of Pennsylvania Press.

Storms, Godfrid. 1975. *Anglo-Saxon Magic.* Folcroft, Penn.: Folcroft Library Editions (reprint of 1948 edition).

Tambiah, Stanley. 1990. *Magic, Science, Religion, and the Scope of Rationality.* Cambridge: Cambridge University Press.

Taussig, Michael. 1993. *Memesis and Alterity—A Particular History of the Senses.* New York/London: Routledge.

Thompson, Robert Farris. 1983. *Flash of the Spirit.* New York: Random House.

Thorpe, Benjamin. 2001. *Northern Mythology.* Hertfordshire, England: Wordsworth Editions in association with The Folklore Society.

Turner, Victor S. 1969: *The Ritual Process.* Ithaca: Cornell University Press.

Wax, Murray and Rosalie Wax. 1962. "The Magical Worldview" in *Journal for the Scientific Study of Religion,* vol. 1: 179–188.

On Magical Runes†
Magnus Olsen
[1916]

I

The runes are, as is well known, the writing system used by the ancient Germanic peoples before they became acquainted with the Latin script at the time Christianity was being introduced. The runic script probably came into existence among the Gothic people(1) in the regions north of the Black Sea in the second century after Christ. It was first and foremost developed from the cursive Greek script, but individual runes were also derived from the Latin alphabet. It came northward with a cultural current from the southeast, and the oldest examples of Nordic runes we know of are from the Danish moor-findings and from contemporary Norse grave-finds from about 200 onward.(2) The runic script is therefore an invention of a Germanic individual within the territory of the Roman Empire. This is the first perceptible expression of Germanic spiritual culture, although, as we shall see, this culture has been influenced by contact with Mediterranean culture. But what aspect of Classical culture is it that brought about the runic script? In what context did the Goths invent the runes in the south near the Black Sea in the time just after the birth of Christ?

Professor Otto von Friesen of Uppsala has provided an answer to this question. This is how he formulated his idea:

The Classical cursive script was used to a great extent epigraphically "as placards and unlearned inscriptions" placed in the plaster of walls, at street corners, in "passages" and gateways, as well as inside the doors of public buildings. Itchy-fingered illiterates, who nevertheless knew how to write, gave free rein to their liveliness and desire for scandal, or notice was being given to one's fellow citizens for another type of practical aim. It is probably the Classical script in this form which Gothic mercenaries learned down in a Roman garrison town or colony on the Danube. Greek was the popular language of the country, Latin was the official language. The inspired Gothic soldiers learned both of these and together with them the Roman and Greek scripts in the form known among their brothers in arms in the barracks. With the help of a fitting development of both alphabets such a Gothic man wrote in his own language. The rune-row was created. Together with the written symbols the Goths also dedicated themselves to Roman forms of military science and the Roman art of war. It was also certainly thanks to their acquaintance with Roman state organization that they were able to form an empire which in the height of this power in the fourth century extended from the Black Sea to the Baltic.(3)

Otto von Friesen strongly emphasizes the practical meaning of the runes in daily life, commercial life and administration. I will not deny that this might have played a role. A detailed investigation of the individual runic signs in their relationship to the Classical models to a certain degree really appears to give von Friesen the right to represent the very oldest history of runic writing– let's say in the first generation, before the runes had spread to other Germanic peoples further away— as he did. But the most important factor, which in my view must be taken into account in connection with the question of the origin of the runes— a factor which von Friesen was not blind to either — is certainly to be sought in an entirely different quarter.

It is a circumstance that I am going to emphasize strongly: already upon its first appearance the twenty-four signs of the runic script form a firmly finished whole. We have independent attestations of rune-rows from Gothic, German and Nordic territories, and it is these attestations that point back to the oldest period of runic writing. The twenty-four runes are organized in a definite ordered series and separated by means of dividing signs into three groups, or "families," each with eight runes. Among the Goths, among the West-Germanic peoples as well as among those living in the North, each rune has its specific name— a word which is otherwise known in the language and which began with the sound of the rune it is supposed to express. Thus **f** is called *fehu* (money), **u** *uruz* (aurochs), **a** *ansuz* (god), etc. So the Gothic, West-Germanic and Nordic runic script is assumed to be derived from one common rune-row with twenty-four signs in a fixed order, divided into three groups and with fixed names, which had been connected to each individual runic sign from the oldest times.

It seems to me as if this fixing of the order of the rune-row took place as a part of the actual creation of the runic script. (I nevertheless concede the possibility of a shorter prehistory, since the Goths wrote with something that was a hybrid of Greek letters and the later runes.) The runes were first and foremost devised to be able to make a firmly established array of twenty-four runestaves.

This could still be considered to be done in this manner for the pedagogical purpose of making the mastery of the runic alphabet easier. The rune-row, the futhark, as we are in the habit of calling it based on the first six runes, would then be a kind of exercise book sample of writing which was convenient to have available. But if we look more closely at the material we find that it definitely contradicts this idea. The rune-row was already known here in the North in the fourth century, attested by a large flat stone (Kylver stone from Gotland) which belonged to a chamber grave. Of what use would exercise book samples of writing be here? And furthermore we know of the futhark on a few small pendants of pressed gold foil, so-called bracteates. Here the rune-row is stamped into the gold plate; someone would have first had to take the trouble to carve the futhark into the stamp. This most obviously indicates that the futhark is something more, and more important than a guide to teaching about writing. The futhark is something in and of itself, it consists of the power of its own contents. It is supposed to accomplish, or have an effect on something— where we find it inscribed on a stone in a grave-chamber or stamped on a gold ornament to be worn around the neck.

Therefore we have come to the the conclusion that the rune-row has an inner power, or a magical power, as it might be called. It is the bound speech of magical signs and magical words, as it can be expressed metaphorically. The futhark is the concentration of the collective magical power of the runes, and in order that these are to be made effective, a certain unalterable ordering must be observed. We only have to think of the comparison with the detailed instructions in the black books for magical signs and magical formulas ("abracadabra," etc.).

Therefore in the futhark we have now found *one* definite type of rune magic. Other groups of magical runic inscriptions are those in which either individual specially employed rune-signs, or the inscription's linguistic content itself, is magical. Usually both kinds are connected in such a way that it can be seen that the first part is a kind of magical formula and the other has one or more runes connected with it which have no linguistic meaning, but rather are exclusively magical signs. As an example we can name the inscription on the Lindholm bog in Skåne:

ek erilaR sa wilagaR hateka:
aaaaaaaaRRRnnn*bmuttt:*alu*:

The Lindholm bone-piece is in all probability an amulet. The magician speaks in the inscription in the first person: "I, Eril, am the wily one (actually: the one who has *vélir*, here to have the tricks of rune-magic in his power)." Thereupon he gives a proof of his magical knowledge in the following line with the 24 magical runes, of which only the last three, **alu** (presumably to express "defense, protection") form any straightforwardly written word.(4)

Above all there are two runes which appear in magical inscriptions: the rune for **t** and the rune for **a**. It is not difficult to find the reason for this: the **t**-rune had as its name the word that designated the god Týr, and the **a**-rune was called **a(n)suR* in Primitive Nordic, i.e. the old word for a god [OE *ōs*, ON *áss*]. When these runes were written the holy divine name contained in them was also manifest and so the inscribing of **t** or **a** was the equivalent to an invocation of Týr or the

Æsir. It is typical to find these two runes repeated several times, or the branches or side-strokes of the **t**-rune will be written three times— as on a bracteate from Zealand (Stephens nr. 57)— probably the equivalent of a triple invocation of Týr.

Between the two types of magical inscriptions, those which consist of the futhark alone, and those which consist of words with linguistic meaning, inscribed for a magical aim, certain connections can be found. Here I shall emphasize such a connection: A rune-magical inscription with linguistic meaning can have its magical power amplified in that the inscription can be divided into groups of twenty-four runes. The number twenty-four is derived from the futhark. Runemasters tried to put 24 runes in each line (as for example the second line of the Lindholm amulet), or one can separate out a section of the inscription containing 24 runes by using a punctuation sign. Sections of 8 runes also appear to play a role.(5) The futhark was actually divided into three parts of eight runes each, and a group of eight runes therefore came to represent one third of the futhark as it relates to its magical content.

Finally I should also mention that the number **10** — for reasons I cannot go into in any more detail here — plays an important role in magical inscriptions with certain contents — and with this we now return to the question of the origin and earliest use of the runes.

What I have already put forward will have given the impression of the great extent to which the runes were used for magical aims in the older Iron Age. However, the inscriptions we have been concerned with up until now have mainly been inscribed on loose objects (amulets). Thus they seem to form a contrast with the inscriptions on the raised "memorial stones," or *bauta*-stones. There is certainly a great deal which suggests that the stone inscriptions also had a specific magical character during the heathen age. On one stone (which had been placed inside a grave) the runes are called "those which stem from the advising powers" (**runo raginakudo** [Noleby 67], which corresponds to *rúnar reginkunnar* in Hávamál 80),(6) and this was certainly the prevailing general conception of the runes. Still it is to be noted that the runic inscriptions in the open air do not, as gravestones of our time do, first and foremost recount who lies buried there in the place in question. The deceased can be named, of course, but he is placed rather in the shadow of the rune-master, who, in several inscriptions makes a great deal of himself. We have stone inscriptions which do not even name the dead man over whom the stone is raised, but merely say that "I N.N. wrote these runes."(7) We have to think that the runemaster, by furnishing the gravestone with an inscription — with the power of the magical effects dwelling in the runes — is directly performing an action by which the grave is sanctified by being placed under divine protection.

All this indicates that in the earliest times, during the heathen age, the runes were something more than a means for written communication. Throughout the entire pre-Christian age the runic script has a side oriented toward the supernatural. The runes are first and foremost a magical script and we can follow this use of them all the way back to the point in time when the Germanic rune-row of twenty-four signs, divided into three groups, was created and provided with names which in part are the names of gods.

The shapes of the runes certainly indicate, as Sophus Bugge and Otto von Friesen have established, that the model of the runic script is to be found mainly among the Greek letters. But is it merely the runic shapes alone which point to an origin outside the Germanic territory? Did the magical elements, which I have so strongly emphasized, first enter the Germanic world along with the arrival of the alphabet? Initially it may seem reasonable that such is not the case. It depends on what the rich Classical material can tell us now.

Here I am quite fortunate to be able to bring to bear an article by the eminent Classical philologist and historian of religion, Albrecht Dieterich, on the subject of "alphabet magic."(8)

Throughout the Mediterranean countries, from which ancient culture spread, one can find a myriad of inscriptions that consist of the alphabet, or parts of it, in connection with other, often incomprehensible, engravings. One can find virtually all of the the old alphabets engraved on vases, lead plates, brick-fragments, urns, marble tablets, rock walls and the walls of houses. There we find the Greek, Latin, Etruscan and the Venetic alphabets. Northward one can encounter this kind of inscription all the way up to the border of the Roman Empire during the imperial age, to the Rhine region. I will cite an example from an urn from Maar near Trier.(9)

First comes the alphabet, upside down. Here I will interject the comment that such upside-down letters, "*stupruner,*" are also known in the North.

After this follow the words ARTUS FUTUTOR and in a new line:
ART LIGO DERCOMOGNI   FUTOTOR

That is: *Art(um) ligo Dercomogni, Artus fututor [est]*. "I consecrate Artus, son of Dercomognus. Artus is '*fututor*'") According to Büchler's translation.)(10)

The word *fututor* designates the inscription as an insulting inscription of malice (*nidinnskrift*), and with the formula "I consecrate" the named person "Artus Dercomognus's son" is here given over to destructive powers. It has to be noted how comprehensive and precise the author of the malicious inscription is in his indication of the person against whom the sorcery is directed: he is the Artus who is the son of Dercomognus.

Besides the alphabet, standing on its head, our attention has to be focused above all on the numerical relationships in the two lines: *art ligno dercomogni fututor*, which works out to twenty-four letters, and in the line just before we have half of that sum, 12 (*artus fututor*). In the second line *art(um)* is abbreviated, because it is supposed to consist of a line of twenty-four signs.

Here there is also some direct comparison to the intended numerical relationships in the runic inscriptions, and both among the Germanic peoples and within the territories of Classical cultures we find that alphabetic magic and intentional numerical relationships are connected. Still more important is the detail that the Greek alphabet, which is used for magical purposes, is the one ancient alphabet with twenty-four signs just like the futhark. And furthermore the special correspondence, which the Pseudo-Tertullian work *Libellus adversus omnes haereses* (possibly by Victorinus Petabionensis, bishop of Pettau in Steiermark at the end of the third century) puts us in a position to discover: *computant ogdoadas et decadas*(11) "they compute by groups of 8 and 10"— is quite like what was demonstrated for the runic system of writing at a time when the Nordic philologists were still unaware of the corresponding links with the cultures of the Mediterranean.

Here it could be proper to conclude the first section of this discussion, which has as its objective the oldest history of the runic script. Where it had previously been the custom to stop the investigation concerning the origin of the runic script, we can now go a step further: The rune-row is formed using the ancient Greek alphabet consisting of twenty-four letters as its model. The futhark was created for a magical purpose, and its division into *ættir*,(12) "*ogdoades*," is due to a Greek influence.

The concept we are expressing here implies that the runes are first and foremost a transplantation into the Germanic territory of the magical script of the South. Therefore we do not need to be so particular about comparing runic forms with those of the letters, but we are aligning the whole inner structure with the ancient alphabet as regards their related applications. With this is also found backing for the runic theory of Bugge and von Friesen, which was placed in a clear historical light by the Swedish archeologists, especially Bernhard Salin.(13)

II

To this point we have been concerned exclusively with the oldest form of runic writing which belongs to the time before the Viking Age, and which used a futhark consisting of twenty-four signs. With the beginning of historical time, around the year 800, there began a new period in runic history, as well as in linguistic history. From now on a rune-row of sixteen signs was used— the special younger, Nordic rune-row. This futhark is also transmitted to us in a fixed order with old traditional names.

Now if there is anything to what was pointed out earlier, that the rune-groups of twenty-four signs constitute an important component in the inscriptions written with the older rune-row consisting of twenty-four signs, then we would expect that from the beginning of the historical time the number sixteen should play a similar role in magical inscriptions to the one played earlier by the number twenty-four. That does indeed bear out. But the number twenty-four is still preserved as the holy number of the runic script long into the Middle Ages right beside the number sixteen.

The best examples of these intentional numerical correspondences in later times are demonstrated - besides the well-known Rök inscription in Östergötland — by a little group of runic inscriptions from around the year 1000 (broadly calculated), which according to its contents must have been carved with a magical aim. They are all carved on loose objects which had nothing to do with grave-goods, and have therefore been removed to places with a dense population, e.g. the towns of Lund, Trondheim, or Sigtuna which were flourishing in the earliest period after the introduction of Christianity. I can not go into details here, but I will content myself with a survey of these inscriptions in transliteration, transcription into the Norse language and translation. To some extent the interpretations are not quite certain.

First we have the inscription I discussed in 1908 in a work entitled "Trylleruneme paa et vævspjeld fra Lund in Skaane":(14)

s k u a r a R : i k i
m a r : a f a: 24 runes
(m) ą n : mn : k r a t:
a a l l a t t i   8 runes

In Old Norse: *Sigvarar-Ingimarr hafa man meingrát.* "Sigvor's Ingimar, he shall have hurtful tears." Followed by 8 magical runes without linguistic meaning.

Additionally, we have the inscription on a weaver's reed of bone from Trondheim ("Et benstykke med Runeskrift fundet i Trondhjem." by S. Bugge and K. Rygh[15]):

```
        5       10      15      20      25      30      35      40
u n a k m æ y i u [i k] u i l a t r i ą æ l n s f u l æ u i f æ k i a h a k ā þ i
```

(Here a section of 32 [2 x 16] runes is divided off at rune 33 ᚴ **k**, which is only half as tall as the other runes. The entire inscription is made up of 32 + 8 runes = 24 + 16. The number 16 appears to be intentional in the section of runes 25-40, which begins with **fu**, which are the first two runes of the futhark. The bind-rune **kā** (r. 38) is therefore intentionally used so that the section of sixteen runes could begin precisely with **fu**.)

According to Bugge, who assumed the inscription reflected poetic meter, this had the following Old Norse linguistic form:
Unna-k meyja,
ek vil-at reą
Erlends fúla víf
ekkja hagaði.

Bugge translated this as follows: "I loved the maid. I do not want to pester Erlend's loathsome wife; as a widow she would be suitable (for me)."(16)

Here we apparently have, as with the magical runes on the weaving temple (which are supposed to cause a person "hurtful tears") to do with an inscription of derision (*nidinnskrift*). The rune-carver intended to injure Erlend and to cause the condition which is intimated in the words "as a widow she would be suitable (for me)."

Finally should be mentioned the poetic inscription on a copper case (used as a container of weights) from Sigtuna. Otto von Friesen read and interpreted this inscription as follows:(17)

fuhul x **ualua** x **slait** x **faluąn** x **fąnkauk** x **ąnąsau(k)a**

(The inscription consists of 40 signs = 24+16 [cf. the previous inscription from Trondheim], if the dividing signs are counted.)

In Old Norse linguistic form and divided into lines of verse:
Fugl *velva(18) *sleit fǫlvan:*
fann gauk á nás auka.

"A bird tore apart the corpse-pale robber; it could be seen by the carrion-cuckoo, how he swelled."

Perhaps future researchers will come along to alter some of this interpretation; but the metrical structure of the inscription and its character as an inscription of derision directed toward anyone who steals the copper case, seems to be clear in any event, and it is only this thing which concerns us in this context.

Of these three inscriptions, the cursing verse of the Sigtuna case makes the greatest demand on our attention. Here we have to do with a two half-line verse in the well-known meter *dróttkvætt*. This has to be liable to arouse thoughts in a certain direction.

The *dróttkvætt* poetic meter is known from hundreds of examples from Old Norse poetry. As a rule it is used in poems composed for the praise of kings and other prominent men; but very frequently *dróttkvætt*-strophes also occur singly as so-called *lausa-vísur*, i.e. improvised verses with their origins in a specific situation. Often these *lausavísur* are of satirical content, sometimes also of such content that they have as their intention to have an effect which is not merely insulting, but also downright harmful ot the person about whom they are composed. These are the real *nid*-verses in *dróttkvætt* meter.

As I became acquainted with the *nid*-inscription in *dróttkvætt* meter on the Sigtuna case, I had to say to myself: In all probability this *dróttkvætt* is not unique with respect to having been carved in runes, if magical power has been amplified by means of the intentional numerical relationships which appear in the grouping of the runes. *Nid* and runes go together in our ancient heathen culture. Therefore should there not also be individual examples of *nid*-poetry which have survived in the literature which were composed in order to be inscribed in runes and which were thus formulated in definite groups of twenty-four and sixteen signs?

Probably the best known of all *nid*-verses are those which Egill Skallagrímsson composes when he is about to leave Norway after having unsuccessfully tried to take possession of an inheritance at a legal assembly (*Gulaþingi*). The saga depicts this in great detail and puts Egill in different situations to improvise a *nid*-verse against Erik Blood-axe and one against queen Gunnhild (*Egils saga* ch. 56–57):

> Svá skyldi goð gjalda,
> gram reki bönd af höndum
> reið sé rögn ok Óðinn,
> rán mins féar hánum;
> folkmýgi lát flœja,
> Freyr ok Njuorðr, af jörðum,
> leiðisk lofða striði,
> landáss, þanns vé grandar.

May the gods drive the king away: thus should they repay him who robbed me of my property; the powers and Odin are angry at him; the land-god, has the oppressor of the people flee from his ground; Frey and Njörð are haters and enemies of the men who violate the sanctuary.

Then Egill steers toward the sea. He sails by an outer coastal fishing station in the fjords, where he learns from some fishermen that the king has outlawed him. Then Egill composed a verse:

> Lögbrigðir hefr lagða
> lindalfs, fyr mér sjölfum,
> blekkir brœðra søkkva
> brúðfang, vega langa;
> Gunnhildi ák gjalda,
> greypt's hennar skap, þenna,
> ungr gatk ok læ launat,
> landrekstr, bili grandat.(19)

The law-breaker determined I would be a long way (from here); the warrior's wife seduces the brother-killer (Erik); that is Gunnhild— her mood is cruel—, whom I have to thank for this banishment; as a young man I could act quickly and repay treacherously any action (against me)."

Then Egill turns back and kills Erik's son Ragnvald and before he leaves the country for good he goes ashore on an island way out in the sea. In the saga it is said: "Egill went up on the island. He took a hazel branch in his hand and went out onto a cliff that faced toward the land. Then he took a horses head and set it up on the pole. There upon he spoke certain words (an incantation) and said: *Here I am setting up a pole of insult* (niðstöngr), *and I direct this **nid** against King Erik and Queen Gunnhild—* with these words he turned the horses head in toward the land— *I direct this **nid** against the landvættir* ("land-spirits") *who dwell in this land, so they will all go astray and none shall reach or find its abode, until they have driven Erik and Gunnhild out of the country.* Then he drove this pole down into a crevice and left it standing there. He also turned the head inward towards the land, and he carved runes on the pole, and they contain that whole incantation. Then he went on board his ship."

The two *nid*-strophes occur in places in the saga's account which might reasonably lead to the mistaken conclusion that they were interpolated here by the discursively narrating saga-writer. To be sure the saga gives no direct indication that the *nid*-poems were inscribed into the *nid*-pole; but according to their contents they were extremely well-suited to constitute 'the whole incantation" (*formála þenna allan*) as the saga says, that it may be ventured to be considered probable that such was the case.(20) Here we are lucky enough to have two different strophes stemming from the same situation. They are among the most powerful *nid*-poems we know of, and if Egill, who was learned in runes, composed them, we can also venture to believe that he took this opportunity to make use of the most powerful rune-magic of which he was a master. It could easily be thought that he endowed the runes with additional power by providing for five groups of twenty-four or sixteen signs or a multiple of these (48, 72, etc.). Such groups could best be formed in *dróttkvætt*-strophes by having each half-strophe (which according to this interpretation constitutes an independent unit) get a specific number of runes, which would have to be a multiplicity of twenty-four or sixteen.

Now let's examine the four half-strophes of the two *nid*-poems. I present them here with the usual tenth century form of runic writing.(21) In the indications of the sounds I try to be completely consistent, as we actually have to do with a master such as Egill. Before **t** and **k** (signifying respectively *t* and *d* as well as *k* and *g*), I leave the *n*-sound unwritten, which corresponds to general practice found in runic inscriptions. I render Norwegian-Icelandic ǫ with **au**, ø with **u** and jǫ with **iu** (not with the less favored long runic cluster **iau**).(22)

The four half-strophes are thus rendered:(23)

(I)   **sua skulti kuþ kialta**   18 runes
        gram riki baut af hautum   20 —
        raiþ si raukn auk uþin   18 —
        ran mins fiaR hanum   16 —

                                          72 runes

        fulkmuki lat fluia   16 runes
        frauR auk niurþr af iurþum 22 —
        laiþis(24) **lufþa striþi**   17 —
        latas þans ui krataR   17 —

                                          72 runes

(II)   **laukbrikþiR hafR lakþa**   20 runes
        litalfs fur miR siulfum   20 —
        blakiR bruþra sukua   17 —
        bruþfag uika laka   15 —

                                          72 runes

        kuniliti(25) **ak kialta**   15 runes
        kraubts hanaR skab þana   20 —
        ukR katk auk la launat   18 —
        latristr bili kratat   19 —

                                          72 runes

The result is surprising: all four half-strophes consist of 72 (= 3 x 24) runes. If we had been dealing with only *one* half-strophe I would not have even noticed this numerical relationship; it could be said that I proceeded in an arbitrary fashion with regard to these passages where the runic writing of the tenth century allowed a variety of orthographies. Furthermore it is significant that one can obtain the same numerical sum in any one of the two half-strophes, which is especially meaningful as a consistent orthography is employed. But in this regard it is important that the individual verse is of such a content that the intended numerical pattern would fit perfectly with it. And now we have here two connected verses (four half-strophes) of just such content: *nid* against the king and queen respectively—where we expect the most magically powerful runes that can be conceptualized. In content the two *nid*-verses against Eirik Bloodax and Gunnhild deviate from all other *lausavísur* in *Egilssaga*. According to the research I conducted I already believe I can say with certainty that they also deviate from all other verses in the saga with reference to their form, i.e. the numerical pattern which they exhibit.(26)

But even more important for the history of Old Norse literature is the fact that Egill's runic *nid*-verses are not isolated examples of intentional numerical correspondences.

It will naturally be seen that for me these two verses have provided impetus to an examination of the oldest Norse poetry keeping, in mind the questions that have been raised here. At present I am in the midst of this investigation, but I can already demonstrate some preliminary results. It appears that the intentional numerical patterns in skaldic verse, which was certainly to be written in runes, occurs especially in *nid*-verses (but as far as I can see this is far from all of them)(27) Other kinds of poetry seem to come into consideration as well, however.

I will give an example which among other things can have some meaning for the question of the interpretation of the obscure Rök inscription.

In northwestern Iceland there lived — at approximately the same time as Egill Skallagrímsson — a man by the name of Vǫlu-Steinn, so named because his mother was a woman who knew magic, a *vǫlva*. This Steinn had two sons, Ogmundr and Egill. Ogmund was killed at the Torskefjord legal assembly and his father was inconsolable over this. Brother Egill then sought out the wise skald Gestr Oddleifsson and asked him for advice on how to console his father (*at fǫður hans bættist helstríð*). Gestr is supposed to have started composing a "Qgumndardrápa," about which nothing more is known. But under Vǫlu-Steinn's name two half-strophes are transmitted in Snorri's *Edda*: in the first a certain Egill, who can hardly be anyone other than Vǫlu-Steinn's son, is called upon to listen to a poem; in the other the poet dwells on the memory of the grave having swallowed up a person who had been dear to him. Konrad Gislason, the great expert on Old Norse skaldic poetry, proposed the appealing conjecture that Gestr began a poem, which Vǫlu-Steinn later continued, to console himself. In such a case the first half-strophe would actually be by Gestr and the second half by the grieving father.(28)

Konrad Gislason interpreted the two half-strophes in the following manner:

1. Heyr Míms vinar mína
   (mér's fundr getinn Þundar)
   við góma sker glymja
   glaumbergs, Egill, strauma
2. Mank þats jǫrð við orða
   endr myrk Danar(29) sendi
   grœnnar grǫfnum munni
   gein Hlǫðvinjar beina.

That is: 1. Egill, heyr mína Míms vinar glaumbergs strauma glymja við góma sker; mér's gefinn fundr Þundar = Egill, hear Óðinn's breast-streams (= the poem) rushing from my mouth; poetic talent has been given to me (or: I have composed a poem).

2. Mank, þats jǫrð gein endr grǫfnum munni við sendi orða grœnnar Hlǫðvinjar myrkbeina Danar = I am reminded, (only all-too-well) that the earth gaped with its wide open mouth toward (in order to swallow) the man (my son).

If these two half-strophes are also put into the runic orthography of the tenth century— here I also left *n* and *m* unwritten before *d* (*t*) and **b** receptively, and I let the final *m* in *grǫfnum* and the initial m in the following word *munni* be expressed with just one **m**, which accords with the old orthographic practices.(30) One once more gets half-strophes in *dróttkvætt* with 72 (3 x 24) letters (line 1.2 has 35, line 3.4 has 37 letters in both):

1. hauR mims uinaR mina
   miR s futr kitin þutaR
   uiþ kuma skar klumia
   klaubarks akil strauma
2. mank þats iurþ uiþ urþa
   atr murk tanaR(31) sati
   krunaR kraufnumuni(32)
   kain hlauþuiniaR baina

In the two strophes of the "Ǫgmundardrápa" it is touching to make the acquaintance of a grieving father who is called to seek consolation in poetry and in this puttering with certain runic groupings. With sheath-knife in hand we can imagine him composing and proceeding tentatively, trying to determine if the words he has chosen fit the intended numerical pattern he wanted to use. Here a great demand is placed on the one who has to be at the same time poet and runemaster— sometimes this can affect the content somewhat, as when Vǫlu-steinn uses a five-part circumlocution for "man." But the demands on stave-count, rhyme and alliteration in no way appear so great that we will have reason to doubt anything about the results I have submitted here.

Vǫlu-Steinn's verse showed us that the runic art could be conjoined with poetry intended to memorialize the dead. Here a statement by Björn Magnússon Ólsen ought to be introduced: "It is possible that the custom prevailing in Iceland of memorializing dead family members and friends with a poem of grief . . . to some extent had replaced or limited the age-old custom of raising runestones in memory of the dead, and that such stones, as a result of this, became more scarce in Iceland than in other Scandinavian countries. If a poem of grief had been composed then a runestone might seem superfluous."(31) Björn Ólsen was without a doubt correct here. Now we can compare Vǫlu-Steinn's memorial poem, intended to have been written in runes, to the great body of texts on runestones that we know from the other Nordic countries. One line of connection leads us over to the Rök stone, which is inscribed with runes in which intentional numerical relationships come out in a multiplicity of ways.(33) Now the Rök-inscription begins with the words: "After Vámod stand these runes; but his father Varin wrote (them) after his son who was consecrated to death." There has been a doubt about the exact context in which the lengthy, and in its content highly peculiar, Rök-inscription was inscribed. I should think we may venture to say that it was to honor a dead person and to protect his resting place. The supernatural power of the runes was used, strengthened by the hallowed number of the futhark.(34)

But Vǫlu-Steinn's poem reminds us even more directly of Egill Skallagrímsson's well-known poem "Sonatorrek" (loss of a son). About this it is said in *Egil's Saga*:

> After Egill Skallagrímsson had been lying in his bed without eating for several days after the death of his favorite son, Boðvarr, his daughter Þorgerðr, who stated she wanted to follow her brother and her father in death, addressed her father and spoke the words that would later become famous: "Now, father, I would like that we should lengthen our lives just long enough for you to compose a dirge for Boðvarr, and I will carve it on a piece of wood (*ek mun rísta á kefli*), and then we can die, if it seems right for us.

There is some controversy as to how this passage in the saga is to be interpreted. Finnur Jónsson, the otherwise so untiring defender of the dependability of the Icelandic traditions, doubts the correctness of what is written here.: This "custom" of inscribing dirges on wooden staves is otherwise not spoken of in the historical sagas, and this use of the runes is certainly an anachronism and only lately included in the saga; perhaps the sentence is an interpolation from the thirteenth century.(35)

A more detailed justification for this interpretation is given by Finnur Jónsson in *Aarbøgr for nord. Oldkyndighed* 1910, p. 292. Initially he points out "it is only in Þorgerðr's verbatim speech that the rune-stick is mentioned, whereas it is not given a single word in the direct narrative of the saga." He goes on to say:

> Next the account itself is not very probable; such a representation of entire poems on staves of wood is otherwise quite unheard of and certainly unhistorical. There is little doubt that the author, or possibly a later editor, has here projected into older times things he was familiar with in his own time, i.e. he knew of pieces of wood upon which individual sentences or short verses were carved, and thought this happened in ancient times as well, and on an even larger scale. In this regard, Þorgerðr's speech has to be considered unhistorical.

I have to remain more conservative with regard to this question than the most zealous defender of the reliability of the Icelandic tradition. A statement such as Þorgerðr's ("you could compose a dirge in memory of Boðvarr, and I will carve it on a stave") precisely reflects in its content the thought which the wise Gestr Oðleivsson gave expression to, and which the grieving father, Vǫlu-Steinn, furthermore put into action. Egill followed Þorgerðr's advice and composed "Sonatorrek," which is still extant. Unfortunately this poem has been transmitted in a very defective state and is in part difficult to understand. How all this could have occurred, whether Þorgerðr really carved it on a stave, and whether this would have then demonstrated any runic art, I can not discuss in any more detail. The latter is unlikely since here the poet and the runecarver could have been the same person.

We are also near the end of the second section of this aspect of the history of runic writing. I will just indicate certain conclusions which we can easily draw from this stage in our still far from completed investigations of the important group of skaldic poems which seem to have been composed with the intention of them being inscribed with runes. At the forefront stand the two strophes in *Egils saga* as the ones that are in every respect the most important.

Egill's two *nid*-verses — in the form they have after they have been transliterated into runic orthography of the tenth century — I would dare to place among the important, but unfortunately rare, *historical runic inscriptions*. Here we have an inscription made up of 4 x 24 runes originating in western Norway during the short span of the years of Erik Bloodax's reign— the most lengthy historical runic inscription we have, about as old as the oldest previously known historical runic inscription, i.e. the memorial stone for Thyre, "the Adornment of

Denmark, (Jelling stone I from 935–40). Since the authenticity of Egill's *nid*-verses (about which no one has ever raised any doubt) is well-established, conclusions in connection with the history of literature can also be drawn in other respects. The two *nid*-verses of Egill in the saga are not transmitted in direct connection with the *nid*-pole. To the contrary, the saga indicates another formula in the prose which is supposed to have been on the *nid*-pole. But since the *nid*-verses have shown themselves to be intended to be written in runes, we can in this way prove that the saga is incorrect on this point. The long prose formula (which is strongly reminiscent of Hávamál 155) is a later addition; it is the *nid*-verses which were inscribed on the *nid*-pole in runes— therefore we have a small contribution to the evaluation of such survivals in the Icelandic family sagas.

Moreover, we should direct our attention to the extremely important linguistic results: If it is regarded as proven that Egill's *nid*-verses were carved with 4 x 72 runes on the *nid*-pole, then it is at the same time established that the West-Norse / Icelandic syncopation is completely carried out by around the year 940, also where -u followed after a short root syllable. Sophus Bugge — who vainly attempted to prove the inauthenticity of the poetry of Brage the Old — defended a slightly divergent interpretation in that he wanted to prove that in Norway it was only after 950 that the older disyllabic forms such as *glaðu* were displaced by syncopated monosyllabic forms with *umlaut*: (glǫð).(36) But Egill wrote — had to write — **kuþ** (*goð*) on the *nid-pole*, not **kuþu**. The latter form requires an additional rune; this can obviously be seen in **baut** (*bǫnd*) in the following line, since this word could still have been represented in runic writing with one vowel sign; but then **hautum** (*hǫndum*) in the same line would also have to be written with one less rune, and then the number 72 would have been lost. Thus we have been able to determine how the letters in a pair of lines in Egill's *nid*-verses appeared. Furthermore, it can be noticed that both he and Gestr Oðleivsson in the "Ǫgmundardrápa" contracted the unstressed verb *er* (*es*) to the preceding word with a loss of its vowel— a corroboration that our linguistic history and metrics are here on the right track at this time.

Furthermore, we should delve a bit more deeply into the cultural-historical side of things: One composed, as I expressed earlier, with a knife in hand and a runestave on one's knee. Gestr Oðleivsson could well have sent the first strophe of the "Ǫgmundardrápa" to Vǫlu-Steinn along with his son Egill, carved on a runestave, and Vǫlu-Steinn continued it— composing and carving the runes. It is certainly more then idle speculation that Egill brought the "rough draft" of his *nid*-inscription against Erik Bloodax and Gunnhild home to Iceland. We actually find precious little literature on runestaves lying around farmer's quarters in Iceland— and therefore our studies have given us a hint toward solving the controversial question "concerning the use of runes beyond their use on monuments."

Here may also be the place to say that we have to give greater respect to the tradition of Norse literature than many historians have done up to now. A real absorption into the old literature, within which trait after trait stands forth and illuminates the other— that is the way to be able to use this literature as a historical source.

And finally I come to the point in this explanation which leads us to the deepest level of our ancient history. I ask the reader ones more to think of Egill Skallagrímsson and Vǫlu-Steinn. To compose poetry and to carve runes was, as Egill Skallagrímsson himself indicates in the "Sonatorrek," the gift of Óðinn to humanity. it can provide consolation in the deepest sorrow. In the "Qgmundardrápa" we are elevated far beyond runes for sorcery into a higher ethical sphere.

†Printed earlier in *Edda* V (1916), pp. 225-245, and as facile II of *Fordomtima*, a series edited by Oskar Lundberg, Uppsala 1917.

Notes

(1) Sophus Bugge, *Norges Indskrifter med de ældre Runer* I p. 143 (1893) Intro. p. 92ff (1905)—cited hereafter as "*NI.*" [As is well-known much has been written about the origin of the runic script and its oldest history in the past twenty years. But none of this touches on the central theme of this article.]

(2) Otto von Friesen, *Om runskriftens härkomst* (Språkvetenskapliga Sällskapets i Uppsala forhandlingar 1904–1906, Uppsala 1904; Sophus Bugge, v. I Intro.; Haakon Schetelig *NI* III, p. 1ff.

(3) Otto von Friesen, *Runorna i Sverige* (Fordomtima I, Uppsala 1915, p. 4ff.) This work is recommended for whoever wants a brief and intelligible survey of Nordic runic writing.

(4) Concerning the inscription of Lindholm (Stephens, *Runic Monuments* I: 219, III, 33) and closely related inscriptions see my explanations in *Aarbøger for nordisk Oldkyndighed* 1907, p. 29ff., in *Festschrift Vilhelm Thomsen dargebracht* (Leipzig 1912), p. 15ff. and in *Bergens Museums Aarbok* 1911, nr. 11 ("En indskift med ældre runer fra Huglen i Søndhordland").—On the reading of the magical runes, in which I follow Sven Söderberg, see my article "Trillerunerne paa et vævspjeld fra Lund i Skaane (Vid. selk. Forhandl. 1908, nr. 7 Kristiana 1908, p. 12 note 2.—[On the interpretation of the Lindholm inscription the reader can now also be referred to *Viking* I (1937), p. 71ff.]

(5) See "Tryllerunerne paa et vævspjeld" p. 19ff.

(6) See Erik Brate's interpretation of the Fyrunga-[= Noleby] inscription (*Arkiv f. nordisk Filologi* XIV, p. 331f.).

(7) Einang-stone in Valdres from the fourth century (*NI*, p. 72ff.).

(8) Albrecht Dieterich, "ABC Denkmäler" (*Rheinisches Museum* LVI 1901, p. 77ff. reprinted in *Kleine Schriften*, p. 202ff.). When it dawned on me that there might be a historical connection between the magical futhark and the Greek alphabet inscriptions, I was as yet not aware that Dieterich in his survey of "ABC-monuments" also names the runic alphabets as discussed in Wimmer's *Runenschrift*. About these he says (87f. [211ff.]: "I cannot say whether the runic alphabets ... have any sort of direct historical connection with the ancient Mediterranean alphabets. That the use of the alphabetic series we have here is the same one that has been established in the Germanic North, will be evident at once. I can provide four definite examples from Wimmer's book..." (cf. Brate, *Östergötlands runinskrifter* v. 2, 1916, p. 170ff.).

(9) *Westdeutsche Zeitschrift* XII 1893, Korrespondenzblatt Nr. 10, p. 201ff.

(10) Dieterich, p. 81 (206) considers Büchler's interpretation to be convincingly correct. Likewise Audollent, *Defixionum tabellae* (Paris, 1904), p. 155. In a later hand the word *aprilis* and some unintelligible

signs have been added to the urn.—[H. Gering (in *Hermes* LI 1916, p. 632ff.) interprets: *art(um) ligo Dercomogni fututor(em)* "I cast a spell on the genital organ of Dercomgnus."]

(11) Ps. Tertullian, *adv. omnes haereses* 15 (*de praeser. haeret.* c. 50). Cf. Schanz, *Geschichte der römischen Literatur* III, p. 344, 437.

(12) This word can be explained as a derivation from the word for "8"; see Erik Brate, *Sv. fornminnesfor. tidskrift* VII, p. 55ff.; cf. Sophus Bugge, *NI* Intro., p. 34, A. Torp Ordavleiding in Hægsed and Torp's *Gamalnorsk ordbok* p. XLIX Sec. 28.2.

(13) In another place I hope to be able to pursue further the suggestions made in this section. [I have not had the opportunity to do this.]

(14) *Christiana Videnskaps-Selskaps Forhandlinger* 1908, nr. 7. The Lund-inscription had been published earlier by Emil Olson (*Fornvännen* 1908, p. 14ff.) with whose interpretations I largely concur. [Others read: "my weeping" (Th. Hjelmqvist in *Studier tillegnade Esaias Tegnér* 1918, p. 388ff.; cf. M. Olsen in *Arkiv for nordisk Filologi* 38 1922, p. 100ff.), "my misfortunes." (Johs. Brøndum-Nielsen in *Nordisk Kultur* VI, p. 139 but *grand* should have been written **krąt**, not **krat**.

(15) Det Kgl. Norske Vidensk. Selk. Skrifter 1901 No. 4 Trondheim 1902. Concerning the numerical relationships, see my work cited in the previous note.

(16) [H. Gering in *Arkiv* 33 1917, p. 63 interprets *Erlendr fúli*'s wife.]

(17) Otto von Friesen, *Fornvännen* 1912, p. 6ff.

(18) Cf. Gothic *wilwa* masc. "robber."

(19) Divergent readings in the manuscripts and divergent interpretations in minor details (cf. Björn M. Ólsen *Arkiv* XIX, p. 107 are meaningless for our purposes.—The *nid*-verses in ES were most recently published by Finnur Jónsson, *Den norsk-islandske Skjaldedigtning* A I, p. 53, B I, p. 46ff.

(20) This interpretation of the relationship between the *nid*-verses and the *nid*-pole in the *Egils Saga* was expressed to me privately by Professor Alexander Bugge, before Otto von Friesen's monograph on the Sigtuna inscription was published.

(21) [On two occasions I was requested to render Egill's *nid*-poems in runes. The first time was in 1922, when Gustav Vigeland wanted to carve these poems on the *nid*-pole which formed part of his sculpture of Egill Skallagrímsson (the runic text was published in an article by Hans Dedekam in *Aftenposten* 1923 nr. 75, 10th Feb., and in Kristian Elster's *Illustreret norsk litteraturhistorie* I, 1923, p. 34). The second time was in 1933, for the use of Sigurður Nordal's edition of *Egilssaga* (plate on p. 163; here, with Nordal, the alternate readings *lǫndum*, first half-strophe 1.2 and *landalfs*, third half-strophe 1.2 were used). After some

vacillation I chose to use the "common" younger runes, but there would have been just as valid a reason to have used runes of the so-called Rök-type. On the occurrence of the two runic types in Norway (and on the Faeroes) in the Viking Age cf. *Nordisk Kultur* VI, p. 85ff. No runic inscriptions are known from Iceland at such an early time.]

(22) A complete parallel to this treatment of ǫ, ø and jǫ is presented by the Hunnestad-stone. Handutgave nr. 104, p. 122ff.): **sautu, laikfruþ, ąsburn**, i.e. *sǫttu, Leikfrøð, Ásbjǫrn*. Additionally, the Jutlandic Bjærregrav-stone II ("Beg. of the 11th cent," Wimmer nr. 46, p. 79ff.) with **auft<i>R, þurbiurn,, miuk**, i.e. *øftiR, Þórbjǫrn, mjǫk*, could be noted.

(23) Since we are only concerned with the sum of letters, I have found it superfluous, both here and in what follows, to differentiate between the two a-runes a and ą, something I otherwise could not have done without a more comprehensive justification.

(24) In the tenth century the form *leiðis* (from **leiðiss*, older *-sR < -seR*), not *leiðisk* was apparently being used, since here the reflexive pronoun is in the dative. Cf. S. Bugge in *Runverser*, p. 117.

(25) Cf. **lantirþi** Wimmer, nr. 48 (Egå, Jutland "ca. 980-90") and **raknhiltr**, nr. 80 and 81 (Glavendrup, Fyn and Tryggevælde, Zeeland from "900–925").

(26) For easily understood reasons relating to the comparative statistical evidence I have gathered to this point (but not yet revised), I place in primary position the other *lausavísur* in *dróttkvætt* which the saga ascribes to Egill, actually 41 whole strophes and one half-strophe. Faced with these 83 half-strophes (cited here according to Funnur Jónsson's *Skjaldedigtning*) one naturally poses the two following questions:

1) Does it often occur that Egill's *dróttkvætt*-strophes, when they are transliterated into runic orthography according to the rules imposed on the two *nid*-verses, contain the same number of letters in both half-strophes?

2) It is a usual situation in Egill's 83 *dróttkvætt* half-strophes that they contain 72 letters when they are transliterated into aforementioned orthography?

Both questions can without a doubt be answered with a definite no. (1) Only in four of the other *lausavísur* in *Egilssaga* (st. 6, 15, 21 and 45) can the same sum of letters in both half-strophes be arrived at without difficulty (these are respectively 69, 71, 75 and 73). (2) The average number of letters in the 83 half-strophes is, when the orthographic method used in the calculation of the two *nid*-verses is used, 69. It is self-evident that the number 72 would have to occur several times (for example in str. 5a. 9b, 24b, 26a, 28a and 32b), just as, for example, 71 and 73 also occur (10 and 4 times respectively thus, as expected, higher and lower numbers accordingly as we get closer to, or further away from, the median, while the number 72 fits in here with its 6 occurrences). The notable thing, however, is that the number 72 is never found in both half-strophes of any one strophe.

(27) Besides it must be remembered here that a good many skaldic poems could have been composed to be written in runes without us being in a position to furnish proof of "intentional numerical patterns." Such numerical patterns could have been aided in many instances (e.g. on the weaving temple of Lund and the weaving reed of Trondheim) by the carver using a bind-rune instead of two runes. Occasionally perhaps dividing signs could also have been counted, such as on the Sigtuna box, according to von Friesen's interpretation.

(28) See Finnur Jónsson, *Den oldnorske og oldislandske litteraturs historie*, I, p. 520, which concurs in Konrad Gislason's interpretation. — "Qgmundardrápa" was most recently published in *Skjaldedigtning* A I, p. 98ff., B p. 93 [cf. E. A. Kock and R. Meissner, *Skaldisches Lesebuch* I (1931), p. 6]. Konrad Gislason's article on the poem's interpretation is found in *Det kgl. danske Videnskabernes Selskabs Skrifter* 5. Række IV (1872) p. 310 and pp. 457-461 (1874).

(29) Perhaps *Dana* should actually be read for *Danar* here" (K. Gislason p. 460).

(30) It is irrelevant in our context if *beina myrk-Danar* are connected. (Ernst A. Kock, *Notationes Norrœnæ* III Sect. 342.

(31) Or **tana** and **kraufnum muni**, if one follows K. Gislason's suggestion mentioned above.

(32) Björn M. Ólsen, *Runerne i den oldislandske literatur* (Copenhagen, 1883), p. 5ff.

(33) See Sophus Bugge, *Der Runenstein von Rök* (Stockholm, 1910), pp. 225ff. with whom I agree in every single point.

(34) Cf. *Arkiv for Nordisk Filologi* 37 1921, p. 230.

(35) *Egils saga*, ed. by F. Jónsson Halle 1894, p. 259 (chap. 78).

(36) Sophus Bugge, *Bidrag til den ældste Skaldedigtnings Historie* (Christiana 1894), p. 21. Cf. Finnur Jónsson, *Aarbøger* 1895, p. 302ff. —Noreen (*Geschichte d. nord. Sprachen*, 3rd ed., 1913, p. 87 considers the time around 900 CE as when syncope had been completed.

Translated by Stephen E. Flowers

The Germanization of Christianity in the *Theologia Germanica*

Glenn Alexander Magee, Ph.D.

I. Introduction: History and Reception of the *Theologia Germanica*

In 1516, Martin Luther discovered a short manuscript in a library in Wittenberg. The manuscript bore no title nor was the name of the author given. When Luther read it, he found himself confronted with a work about which he would later write, "Next to the Bible and Saint Augustine no other book has come to my attention from which I have learned—and desired to learn—more concerning God, Christ, man, and what all things are."(1) That same year, he had the text printed under the title *Eyn Deutsch Theologia*. It has come to be known simply as *Theologia deutsch*, and, more commonly, by the Latinized title *Theologia Germanica*. Luther wrote a short introduction to accompany the text. He subsequently discovered a longer version of the work, known today as the Würzburg manuscript, and had that printed (with a longer introduction) in 1518. Numerous editions appeared during Luther's lifetime, and some two-hundred have been printed since.

We know that the *Theologia Germanica* was probably written in the middle of the fourteenth century, and although we still do not know the name of the author, we know that he belonged to the Teutonic order. The order was divided into three groups: knights (all members of the German nobility), priests, and serving brothers. The author of the *Theologia Germanica* was a priest.(2) After the Crusades the order, whose headquarters was in Frankfurt am Main, turned its attention to combating heresy and treating the sick.

The fourteenth century in Germany is often referred to as the "century of heresy."(3) The cultural and political situation that made possible this flowering of heresy is complex. The bitter conflict between Louis of Bavaria and Pope John XXII over the Church's attempts to assert absolute sovereignty over European political order led to Louis's invading Rome and installing his own "counter pope." Pope John responded with the "Interdict" of 1324 excommunicating Louis and all those loyal to him. This created a social crisis, the magnitude of which can hardly be overstated. Louis encouraged his subjects to ignore the Interdict, but the nobles, clergy, and laity nevertheless split into those loyal to the Pope and those loyal to Louis. This event became a watershed for dissatisfaction with the Church and its doctrines, and the laity felt emboldened to criticize the Church and even to break from it altogether. Clergy frequently did not minister in localities which had proclaimed their loyalty to Louis and, as a consequence, for years large areas of Europe received little religious instruction. The influence of the Church began to wane, and its doctrines came more and more to be challenged. The necessity of an organized church itself was even questioned by many. Individuals began to form private religious associations which became the forerunners of the later "pietist" movement in Protestantism. These associations took on a decidedly mystical character, emphasizing individual salvation through union with God. Church dogmas concerning original sin, the sacraments, and the intercessory role of the clergy were not so much rejected as forgotten or ignored.

Many of these heretical Christians identified themselves as the "Friends of God" (*Gottesfreunde*). The *Theologia Germanica* opens with the words, "God the Almighty has spoken this little book through a wise, thoughtful, genuinely righteous person, a friend of His." These words were thought to have been written either by the author himself, or by another close to him. The "Friends of God" movement was characterized by an emphasis on individual salvation through detachment from the ego and from worldly ambition, but also by an insistence on the importance of an organized church and external rules and observances. The *Theologia Germanica* is essentially a brief primer on the mystical theology of the Friends of God. The influence of Meister Eckhart (ca. 1260–ca. 1327) is readily apparent.

The arch enemies of the Friends of God were the so-called "Brothers and Sisters of the Free Spirit." It is our anonymous author's frequent attacks on the "Free Spirits" which help us to date the text to the mid-fourteenth century. The Free Spirits believed that since God himself is beyond good and evil, and not subject to law, human beings come closer to Him through the rejection of all laws and external constraints, including ethical commandments. The roots of their extreme views are to be found in the apocalyptic visions of men like Joachim of Fiore (1135–1202), who promised a coming age, the Age of the Holy Spirit, in which the organized church would simply wither away.

Surprisingly, the Catholic Church did not get around to condemning the *Theologia Germanica* until 1612, by which time it had been translated from Middle High German into Latin. Despite Luther's admiration for the work, its reception among Protestants was mixed. Calvin, for example, condemned the work. Over the years, the *Theologia Germanica* picked up an unusual array of admirers, including the philosopher and biographer of Hegel, Karl Rosenkranz.

II. What is German in the *Theologia Germanica*?

The *Theologia Germanica* is a Christian mystical work of great depth, filled with profound insights which can serve as a source of inspiration and ethical guidance for non-Christians as well. The reason for this is that there is actually very little in it that is specifically Christian. Most of the features of traditional Christianity that tend to irk non-believers (the insistence on guilt arising from original sin, the denigration of nature and the body, the emphasis upon suffering and calamity, etc.) are wholly absent from the work.

My thesis is that this is because the *Theologia Germanica* belongs to the ongoing history of the "Germanization" of Christianity. This is the process by which Christianity was assimilated by the Germanic peoples through a sometimes radical alteration of Christian teaching to suit traditional Germanic religious attitudes, mores, folk beliefs, and customs. The process is thought to have taken place during roughly the period 350–1100, but the argument can be made that a tension between the Near Eastern ideology of Christianity and Germanic culture persisted, and that the Germanization of Christianity has continued, in one form or another, until the present day. This history is analyzed extensively by James Russell in a 1994 work entitled *The Germanization of Early Medieval Christianity*.(4)

To explain how and why the *Theologia Germanica* fits into the history of the Germanization of Christianity, I must give a general account of that history itself, and attempt to arrive at certain conclusions about what is essential about the pagan, Germanic *Weltanschauung*. I can then argue for how that *Weltanschauung* resurfaces in the *Theologia Germanica*.

The period of the conversion of the Germanic peoples to Christianity began with a few Visigoths in the fourth century, at a time when Christian dogmas were just beginning to be established and codified. This means that when the Germans first encountered Christian beliefs, those beliefs were in a fluid, evolving state. It also helped that Germanic religion was not characterized by an insistence on belief in certain claims, or adherence to a set creed. Therefore, at least in one way it was easy for the Germans to convert since they tended to regard the *details* of Christian dogma as unimportant.(5) This attitude is still reflected, centuries later, in the writings of the German mystics and in the *Theologia Germanica*. Eckhart, Tauler, and our anonymous author (as well as later mystics such as Jacob Boehme) profess beliefs which are at odds with traditional Christianity, yet if they are aware of the conflict they seldom mention it or attempt to justify themselves. It is as if they regard doctrinal issues as relatively unimportant.

The difficulty in converting the Germans to Christianity was that they did not have any immediate spiritual needs which Christianity could minister to. According to the Germanic cosmology, the world originates in the murder of a primal being (Ymir) by three of his offspring. Thus, the cosmos owes its existence to an original crime. However, the guilt for this crime remains with the god Odin who, along with his brothers, did the deed; it does not transmit to humanity. The concept of an "original sin" infecting humankind was therefore completely foreign to the Germans. Needless to say, the bellicose Germans also found Christianity's ethical doctrines rather hard to stomach. In Nietzsche's terms, the ancient Germanic religion was "life affirming," in that it celebrated worldly success, strength, and health. Christianity was "life denying" in that it tended to denigrate those very values, and to set another, higher existence over this one. Russell essentially employs this same distinction when he writes of the contrast between Germanic religion and Christianity as a contrast between "world affirming" and "world rejecting" religions.(6) In sum, the religion of the Germans and Christianity seemed utterly opposed.

Christian missionaries solved this problem simply by misrepresenting Christianity. Missionaries tended to emphasize temporal rewards which would be conferred by God upon those who accepted the Christian faith.(7) Some even portrayed Christ to the Germans as a noble warlord! In addition, they attempted to subtly redefine German virtues to move them closer to Christian ideals. The warlike nature of the Germans was not always seen as an impediment to their conversion. Pope Gregory the Great, for example, was a supporter of the use of warfare to spread Christianity, and saw that German ferocity could be an advantage to the Church.(8) Indeed, one can see the phenomenon of the Crusades as largely a "Germanic" approach to spreading the faith: the *wut* or fury of the Berserker unleashed in the name of the Lamb of God. The chivalry of the medieval, Christian knight is also a natural outgrowth of a pagan, German ethos.

But the Germans would never feel quite comfortable in Christian dress. They could never truly embrace the message of the Sermon on the Mount. And so they wound up changing Christianity to suit themselves. Unwilling to give up their traditional festivals, they simply gave them a Christian veneer. And so Yule, complete with the log, the tree, and the mistletoe, became the festival of the birth of Christ. The festival of the goddess Ostara became "Easter," the commemoration of the death and resurrection of the Savior. Over the course of centuries, Christianity was transformed into, for all intents and purposes, a Germanic folk religion.(9)

Furthermore, since they found the literal message of the Gospels so foreign and distasteful, the Germans insisted they couldn't mean *just* what they said, and so were born the countless heresies of the Germanic (and Celtic) Christians, as well as Christian mysticism.

The tradition of German mysticism is rich and varied, but at its core is an insistence upon the necessity of detachment and ego-nullification. The German mystics continually insist that in order to come to God we must detach ourselves from worldly things, and especially from the ego and its appetite for its own aggrandizement. Such a doctrine is not, of course, exclusive to German mysticism. It is, in fact, universal. However, some versions of this doctrine emphasize withdrawal from worldly affairs, and even exhort the aspirant to go "beyond good and evil" and set aside any idea of ethical obligation. This approach is quite foreign to the mainstream of the German mystical tradition. German theology, philosophy, and mysticism tend to exhibit a characteristic which has come to be part of the stereotype of the German character itself: an almost masochistic zeal for doing one's "duty," and a mania for order and regulation.

Where does this tendency come from? At first glance, it seems rather hard to square with our image of the wooly German barbarian, who seemed to live for imbibing vast quantities of mead and generally wreaking havoc everywhere he went. Yet there is a continuity here, beneath the surface. As I have already noted, under Christianity German bellicosity found an outlet in the Crusades. But after the Crusades, where was it to express itself? Many of the knightly orders that had fought in the Crusades—like the Teutonic Order of our anonymous friend—were converted essentially into charitable organizations. What became of the fierce *wut* of the Berserker? There is no single answer to this question. But in the case of some men it was *turned inwards*, toward the self, rather than outwards, toward the battlefield. What we find in the German mystics and philosophers—down to the present age—is a call to arms against the greatest adversary of all: the intransigent, appetitive, sinning ego. The human soul, the interior man, becomes the new battlefield.

One can discern a similar pattern among other Indo-European peoples. The Buddha, as is well known, was not a Brahmin but a Kshatriya, a member of the Indian warrior caste. He taught a doctrine of self-mastery involving meditation, control of the mind, and an "eightfold path" which enjoined right action, right mindfulness, right livelihood, etc. Such a life requires the "spiritedness" of a warrior—what the Germans called *wut*, and the Greeks called *thumos*—directed inward, in a military campaign to subdue the self. It involves a ferocious discipline and self-control that strike the ordinary, appetitive man as an unhealthy extremism.(10) The *thumotic* nature of Buddhism became fully manifest in its Japanese incarnation. It is no accident that Zen became so closely tied to the Japanese warrior caste, the Samurai, and that it is associated with the martial arts of archery and fencing. To this day, Zen monks lead lives that would seem quite familiar to the average Marine recruit, even undergoing a "hell week" of round-the-clock meditation.

As I shall discuss in the next section, this martial ideal of self-mastery and other warrior virtues are readily apparent in the *Theologia Germanica*. One can also find the "life-affirming" or "world-affirming" character discussed earlier. Even more interesting are the appearance of what Jung would no doubt call "archetypes" of the collective German unconscious, which appear when our author attempts to use an image to explain his Germanized Christian teaching. Finally, one can discern, in germinal form, ideas which would later flower in the philosophies of thinkers like Kant, Fichte, Schelling, Hegel, and Heidegger.(11)

III. A Brief Commentary on Key Passages in *Theologia Germanica*

(a) The Relation of God to Creation

The *Theologia Germanica* teaches a doctrine of *panentheism*, which literally means "all-in-God-ism." Our author asserts that the Perfect, or God, comprises all beings, or that all beings are in it. Now, the word panentheism looks quite a lot like the more familiar *pantheism*, so much so that careless readers often confuse them. Pantheism, or "all [is] God-ism," is the position that God is in all things, or that all things just are God. But not only do the words tend to blend together, but the concepts behind them tend to blend also. So, at various times, our author speaks as if all things are in God, and at other times speaks as if God is in all things. To literal minds, this looks like a contradiction. To the mystical mind, these are two equally legitimate ways of approaching the same phenomenon. Chapter One states, "The Perfect is a Being who has comprised and embraced in Himself and in His Being all that is. Without this Being and outside of it there is no true being and in it all things have their being since it is the core of all things."(12)

The Perfect is not identifiable with any of its "parts" or the things which it embraces, since none of these is perfect.(13) The text explicitly states that there is no true being outside the Perfect, or God, and that true knowledge is knowledge of the "whole," not of its parts. In a later chapter we read, "All knowledge limited to separate parts will come to naught when the Whole is perceived" (*Also wird auch alle Erkenntnis der Stücke zunichte, wenn das Ganze erkannt wird*).(14) We have here on the one hand what resembles a Platonic conception of wisdom as knowledge of the whole, and on the other something approaching a Hegelian conception of beings as "moments" of the Absolute.

Furthermore, in perennial mystical fashion we are informed that the Perfect is nameless "because it is not any created thing." Here our author comes close to stating Heidegger's "ontological difference": Being is not *a* being; it is not itself a thing, and thus it is no-thing. In

Chapter Thirty-Four he states, "[God] is the being of all beings [*Gott ist aller Seienden Sein*], the Life of all living things and the Wisdom of the wise. All things have their being [*Wesen*] more truly in God than in themselves and in their own powers, life, and other endowments."(15)

(b) The Role of the Negative, and the Inherent Goodness of Creation

It is a well-known fact that one of the differences between monotheistic and polytheistic religions is that in monotheism the "devil," or negative principle, is usually excoriated and made totally separate from the divine. Under polytheism, notably Hinduism, the negative is regarded as a necessary moment of the whole, and of the divine. In the *Theologia Germanica*, the devil is seldom mentioned. The author connects him to the ego: "The concerns of the I and the self are the devil's field. That is why he is the devil. My many words on the subject can be summed up by a few: Cut off yourself, cleanly and utterly."(16) The devil is here identified as that which cuts us off from God. However, later we are told that "The devil is good as part of existence" (*der Teufel ist gut, indem er ist*). In other words, the devil too is within God, and all that is within God is, in a way, good. The very next sentence reads: "You cannot in that sense say that anything is evil or bad." The author then states that sin is "to intend or desire or love differently from God and that kind of willing is not a part of being. Therefore it is not good."(17) To turn away from God is the only evil. However, if the devil exists then even he is part of the whole, and thus, in a way, good. In Chapter Fifty-Five, the author states: "When one holds to the best that one can discern in creatures, keeps to it, and does not turn back, one gradually arrives at something better, and even better until one can know and taste that the eternal Goodness is a perfect Good, without measure, without number, above all goods in created form."(18)

The pagan, "world-affirming" character of the text is evident in Chapter Forty-Seven, when the author states that the world is paradise: "But what is paradise? All things that are, for everything that is, is good and pleasing—yes, pleasing also to God. Therefore creation should be termed what it is, namely, a paradise." The topic of self-will as turning from God is then broached again: "In this paradise all things are lawful save one tree and the fruit thereof. This means: In all that exists around us nothing is forbidden, nothing is basically contrary to God, save one thing. That one thing is self-will [*Eigenwillen*], or to will and intend otherwise than the eternal Will wills."(19) This may seem as if the author is permitting mankind a great deal of license, as the Brothers and Sisters of the Free Spirit do. In fact, however, he apparently believes that all immorality can be understood as self-will. As is the case with so much of what the text has to say about morality, this position is proto-

Kantian. Immorality has its origin in separating oneself from what can be willed universally (the "eternal Will") and thinking that one gets to "play by one's own rules," which is "self-will."

(c) The Ego and Self-Will

A word must be said about the sense in which terms like "ego," "I," and "self" are used in the *Theologia Germanica* and in mysticism in general. Critics of mysticism, especially those who come at it from a eudaimonistic ethical perspective, tend to be horrified by mysticism's assertion that we must destroy the ego and selfishness. But what must be understood is that by "ego" the mystics do not typically mean our sense of personality or individual identity as such. What they mean is the rather narrow, impoverished sense of "self" that most human beings exhibit: a self identified with appetites and desires, and also with such trivia as social status and worldly power; a self that is more Id than Ego. The mystics do not typically enjoin us to destroy our personhood, but rather to relinquish the attachments which stunt the growth of our personhood and make it narrow and small. This is what is meant by annihilating "ego."

The author quotes St. Paul saying that when the Perfect comes, the partial and imperfect is "done away with." He then asks when the Perfect comes, and answers "I say, when it is known and felt and tasted in the soul to the extent possible."(20) One must keep in mind the different equivalencies the author has set up: the Perfect = (true) Being = the nameless = God. So our author is telling us that God comes when He is "known and felt and tasted in the soul." The "coming of God" is not presented here as an historical, worldly event, yet to occur. Rather, it occurs, or can occur, in the soul of each, single man. How can this happen? In brief, the *Theologia Germanica* teaches that it happens when we *make a space* in the soul for God to enter in, by thwarting ego.

Our author writes, "For in whichever creature this perfect life is to be known, creatureliness, createdness, selfishness, must be abandoned and destroyed." He later adds to this litany "impulse-ridden desire" and states, "As long as one holds to these things and is cemented to them, the Perfect remains unknown."(21)

What then is sin (*Sünde*)? Sin is "nothing but a turning away on the part of the creature from the unchangeable Good toward the changeable."(22) In Chapter Three, we are told that Adam fell because of "his presumption and because of his I and his Mine, his Me and the like." Further, his sin did not consist in the *act* of eating the forbidden fruit. Rather, his sin consisted in the *intention* or the mental attitude with which he did the deed. Our author writes that "He could have eaten seven apples, yet had this not been connected with his presumption, he would not have fallen."(23) In short, he ate the fruit of the Tree of Knowledge with a view toward self aggrandizement, and this, not the actual taking and eating of the fruit, is his sin. In this "presumption" he acts to glorify himself purely for its own sake, and so turns away from God. To put it another way, Adam is a "part" of the whole or the perfect, having his being only in the Perfect. In acting selfishly, he acts so as to make his "partial" nature itself an independent whole; to break off his part from God. But this can only lead to sickness and ruin. Just as an organ of the body cannot thrive or live apart from the whole organism, neither can a creature thrive and live when it tries to abstract itself from the divine unity. A selfish soul shrivels and dies when it separates itself from God.

(d) The Kinship of Man and God

How is the fall of man to be redeemed? The *Theologia Germanica* states, "Man could not do it without God and God has not designed to do it without man. Hence God assumed human nature or humanity. He became humanized and man became divinized." Now, this sounds straightforwardly like a description of the Incarnation: in order to expiate the sins of mankind, God assumes human form as Jesus Christ. The doctrine of the Church was, and is, that this happened one and only one time, in the person of the Nazarene. Mystical German Christianity asserts, however, that it can happen in us all. Thus, in the very next passage, the language of which parallels what was just quoted, our author writes that his own fall "must be amended in the same way. I cannot do it without God, and God does not command or will it without me. For if it is to happen, God must become humanized in me. This means that God takes unto Himself everything that is in me, from within and from without, so that there is nothing in me that resists God or obstructs his work."(24) One finds a similar doctrine in Eckhart, and it was for this doctrine that he was censured.

A feature of the pre-Christian Germanic worldview was a belief in an "organic" connection between the gods and mankind.(25) The gods created the human race by endowing two trees named Askr and Embla with divine spiritual qualities. As in Greek mythology, the gods also literally propagated human beings from time to time. In fact, it was common for Germanic royalty and nobility to trace their genealogy to Odin. There is thus no sharp, ontological divide between the human and divine. The difference is actually more a matter of degree than of kind. Christians are asked to believe, on faith, in the Incarnation as an historical event, and to believe, again on faith, in a Second Coming yet to happen, also understood as a literal event. The speculative mind rebels against such claims and insists that if it *must* believe in this doctrine, then it will have to find an inner, personal meaning in it. In other words, it chooses to take the story of the Incarnation as myth, rather than as historical report. The Germanic speculative mind read in this story a representation of the organic connection of man to God. Christ, the German mystics claim, was not unique. He was Everyman. We are all the sons of God. In our innermost being, we are all organically one with the divine. But our selfishness, our *Ichheit*, keeps us from realizing this. In Chapter Fourteen, the author states that it is possible for man to come so close to the life of Christ that "he can be called—and can in fact be—godly and divinized."(26)

(e) The Sacrifice of the Worldly Eye

Chapter Seven of the *Theologia Germanica* states that "the soul of Christ has two eyes, a right eye and a left eye." The right eye of Christ was turned "toward eternity and the Godhead and therefore immovably beheld and participated in divine Being and divine Wholeness." This vision of eternity remained constant in spite of all temporal events that afflicted him. But what of the left eye? It was turned precisely toward the outer world of space and time. It "penetrated the world of created beings and there discerned distinctions among us, saw which ones were better and which ones were less good, nobler or less noble." Thus, the left eye "was involved in a full measure of suffering, distress, and travail." The text goes on to say that the "outer man" experienced the sufferings of the cross, while the "inner man" and the "right eye" remained "unmoved, unimpeded."(27)

Our author goes on to state that the "created soul of man" has these two eyes, one focused upon time, the other on eternity. One might take this to mean that in order to come to God, or to have God come to be in us, we must, while keeping an eye on worldly affairs, at the same time remain cognizant of eternity and of the Perfect. However, the author is very clear that he does not mean this. He states that these two eyes cannot function simultaneously. "If the soul is looking into eternity through its right eye, the left eye must cease all its undertakings and act as if it were dead." If not, then the left eye, with its focus upon worldly things, would hinder the activity of the right.(28) However, the Würzburg manuscript goes further than this. It states, "Therefore, he who desires the one, must relinquish the other. For no one can serve two masters" (*Darum, wer das eine haben will, der muss das andere lassen fahren. Denn es kann niemand zweien Herren dienen*).(29) In other words, in the language of the metaphor, one must relinquish the left eye with its worldly focus.

In considering this unusual account, it is difficult to avoid thinking of the tale of how Odin sacrificed an eye in order to drink from Mimir's well. Accounts of the myth do not specify which eye, but this hardly matters. Drinking from the well gave Odin complete wisdom in the form of an insight into the *ørlög* (in Old High German *wurd*, in Old

English *wyrd*): the fate or destiny of all things, as determined by all that which has been laid down in the past. In modern German, "the past" is *die Vergangenheit*, the foregoing-ness; hence the guardian of the well is Mimir, "memory." Having drunk from Mimir's well, Odin was even able to see how the gods themselves would come to their end. But in gaining this insight, Odin lost something as well: the ability to see existing things as having any lasting value or significance, and, therefore, to involve himself with the affairs of the world in a wholehearted way. This is what the loss of the eye represents. Wisdom involves an insight into the ephemeral nature of everything. On gaining it, one can no longer see things in the same way. One can no longer have trust or faith in things as they appear. Odin's inner eye is opened to the eternal pattern of the cosmos, yet his "outer" vision, his ability to regard worldly things, is crippled. The author of the *Theologia Germanica* exhorts us to lose our worldly eye, and to open the other to the *ørlög*, the ur-law of the cosmos now become the *logos* of John.

(f) An Ethics of Detachment and Surrender

So, to summarize what has been laid down so far, to come to God means for God to come into us, to become, in a sense, the incarnation of God. How do we do this? By canceling selfishness and egocentricity: we must turn our focus from worldly things to the eternal. If we accomplish this, then we make a space in the soul for God to enter in. This is all well and good, but we are still embodied beings, interacting with other beings. Our author does not enjoin the life of a hermit and he certainly does not advocate suicide. So, how do we live? How can one live having given up the "eye" that deals with the world? Our author offers a traditional, mystical answer, involving essentially two components: (1) we will still deal with things, though in a detached manner; and (2) when we act, we will act out of disinterested respect for law, not according to ego. I will discuss each of these in turn. The first element will emerge as strikingly Heideggerean, the second as strikingly Kantian.

Chapter Seventeen of the *Theologia Germanica* enjoins an ethics of detachment: "As long as a person attaches high regard to something or treats something with preference in his love, opinion, desire, or urge—things of the varied world, that is, his own self or whatever—he will not attain [the true life in Christ]."(30) But how do we effect this detachment? The text instructs us that we can do this not by renouncing things but by surrendering to them. Chapter Twenty-one opens, "We are told about other ways of preparation. One says we should submit to God, in obedience, in carefree serenity [*Gelassenheit*] and subjection."(31) *Gelassenheit* is a term used by Eckhart, later resurrected by Heidegger, who consciously drew on Eckhart. Translating literally, one could render it as leaving-ness, letting-alone-ness, allowing-ness, or letting-be-ness. Translators of Heidegger usually render it "letting beings be." What it means for the author of the *Theologia Germanica* is that we submit to God by submitting to *everything*. This follows logically, since we have been told that God contains all. Our author writes that if we are to yield to God in such stillness we must at the same time be subject to everything, including not only God but also ourselves and all created beings, nothing barred. If you want to be obedient, serene [*gelassen*], and submissive to God, you must also be serene, obedient, and submissive in relation to the created world around you, in a spirit of compassionate yielding, and not in a spirit of busyness.(32)

"In the spirit of busyness" is a felicitous translation, for what is the spirit of business? Regarding things in terms of their utility, as objects to be consumed or otherwise used, or exchanged. It is a self-centered standpoint, in that it determines the value of objects solely in relation to the self. In a later chapter we read, "We must, by the power of divine truth and righteousness, be subject to God and all creatures and no single thing and being should be subject to us."(33)

Now, this is the sort of thing that would be grist for Nietzsche's mill. What a fine statement of "slave morality"! What is important to understand, however, is that this ethics of surrender is actually a way towards *mastery* over all things. If we attach ourselves to things, and fight, oppose, and resist this or that, then we are subject to those things. But in surrendering to the whole, "in a spirit of compassionate yielding," we advance to a point where things can no longer hurt or affect us in any fundamental sense. And, at the same time, having opened ourselves to the whole, *we have opened ourselves to God.*

(g) An Ethics of Law and Duty

There is another aspect to the ethics of the *Theologia Germanica*, however, aside from detachment, and that is law. To draw another parallel to Indian thought, in the *Bhagavad-Gita*, the warrior Arjuna is taught by Krishna to view the carnage of war, and life itself, in a detached manner. The question arises, however, how a detached man should act in the world, if he intends to go on living. The answer Krishna gives is that one acts according to duty. In the case of the Kshatriya, that would mean acting according to the specific duty of his caste. The detached warrior is guided by duty, without thought for the fruits of his actions, and the performance of duty reinforces his detached standpoint. The *Theologia Germanica* teaches a similar doctrine: detachment does not lead to lawlessness, but to the disinterested performance of duty for its own sake. In the *Theologia Germanica*, however, "duty" has been generalized, in the main, to become a universal "moral duty" binding on all human beings, rather than the duty of a specific social group. There are hints, however, that our author's conception of virtue is heavily influenced by an ideal of knightly conduct that would probably have been instilled to some degree in all members of the Teutonic order. I will deal with these hints later.

The Brothers and Sisters of the Free Spirit believed that detachment does, in fact, lead to lawlessness, and this is the chief reason why the author of the *Theologia Germanica* continually attacks them. In Chapter Five he writes, "Not a few argue that man before God should become free from rules, will, love, knowledge, and so on."(34) In Chapter Sixteen, he refers to the life the Free Spirits advocate as "most sweet and most pleasant to nature, self, and the I. . . . In many people it becomes the extreme of wickedness."(35) In other words, the Free Spirits adopt their way of life thinking that it is a way of coming to God, but in fact it is merely a way in which the ego can covertly reassert itself. It is a rationalization for self-indulgence. The temptation toward ego aggrandizement is present in all human beings. Our author writes that "because of this inclination, it becomes necessary and useful to have order, rules, law, and commands. Law and command make our blindness evident to us and constrain wickedness into order." ("Law" must be understood very broadly here, to mean the laws of society, moral rules, and customary restraints on behavior of all kinds.) He continues that without such restraints "people would be much more wicked and undisciplined than dogs and cattle." Laws and rules help turn many toward the truth, by restraining the baser parts of their nature. Indeed, the man who could find the truth and perfect his soul without guidance from law is extremely rare. Therefore, laws must not be scorned. "The rules are an appeal to those who do not know any better, to come to the truth so *that they may know and inwardly recognize the reason for all laws and all order*."(36) This last part is significant: our author does not want to breed automata, mindlessly obeying rules. He wants men to internalize moral and spiritual law, to live with law so intimately that it becomes a part of them. Then they can come to recognize why the laws are laws, and why they are necessary.

When one has achieved this standpoint, then one is no longer moral because one is afraid of punishment, or desirous of social recognition, or desirous even of divine reward. The text states "The illumined ones live in freedom. This means that they are free from fear of pain or hell. They have abandoned hope of reward or heaven. They live in pure surrender and obedience to the eternal Good, in love that frees."(37) Later, the text states, "Where this [pure surrender and obedience] happens, the outer man is structured and tutored by the inner man, and learns that no outward law or teaching is needed."(38) In short, the illumined man is capable of giving a law to himself; he no longer needs a law to be imposed upon him externally. Further, he follows the self-imposed law purely for the sake of following the law or doing the good, without an ulterior motive. The illumined man "wills and loves nothing but for the sake of the Good, for no other reason but its goodness. He does not will and love because the circumstance is a particular one or because it is good for this or that purpose, pleasure or pain, joy or sorrow, sweetness or bitterness, or similar contrasts. He does not choose to take such questions into consideration, least of all not on behalf of the self or as a self."(39)

(h) Pagan, Aristocratic Virtue

The "Teutonic" character of the *Theologia Germanica*'s ethical teaching surfaces when our author expresses his attitude towards those who seek some reward for virtuous conduct. He states that "the person who leads a life in Christ with the intention of obtaining some use or earning some glory from it embraces this life as a hireling who is out for recompense and not from love; he possesses none of Christ's life. He who is not devoted to it out of love has no part of it."(40) In contrast to the "hireling" (*Löhner*), who approaches the "life in Christ" with avarice, the illumined man is portrayed as a spiritual knight, who has embraced the good out of a selfless sense of duty, and pursues it come what may, without thought for the consequences, and least of all for reward.

In Chapter Twenty-Six, the author presents a short list of virtues that will be exhibited by the man in whom God has come to be: "To this life [in Christ] also belong reputable behavior, rectitude, consistency, truthfulness, and everything else pertaining to virtue in human relations. Such things must be there. Where they are not, something has gone wrong with the union [of man and God]."(41) The virtues the author chooses to mention explicitly (rather than consign to the category of "and everything else pertaining to virtue") are significant. All four are fixtures of the ethos of chivalry. The primary virtue mentioned is truthfulness (*Wahrhaftigkeit*). To be "true" means more than simply to speak the truth, it means to be constant, and to *be* rather than merely to seem. The "true" man exhibits consistency (*Gleichmäßigkeit*), because there will be no conflict between his words and his deeds, and no other way in which he is divided against himself. The inconsistent man presents an appearance of being or thinking one way, but then surprises us by showing a very different character in other circumstances. He is thus "untrue," in a fundamental sense. The man of rectitude is the morally conscientious man, the man who is concerned with the rightness of his actions. This is also a form of being true: rightness or justice involves correctly fitting actions to circumstances and to people.

The man of rectitude must recognize others for what they *really* are and reward or punish appropriately. Injustice is a denial of truth, for it involves treating others as what they are not, as when an innocent man is punished for a crime he did not commit, or another is rewarded for something he did not actually accomplish. Finally, behaving reputably is the most straightforwardly chivalric of the four virtues. To be concerned with reputable behavior is to be concerned with what one is reputed to be. One must behave in such a way that the story others tell about one is honorable and admirable. In truth, one must create this story through one's actions. This virtue is inescapably social, and inescapably pagan and aristocratic.

When the *Theologia Germanica* gives specific advice about how to start on the way to illumination, it reads like advice intended for an apprentice knight. The author specifies four things:

Needed in the first place is keen yearning for, diligence in, and steadfast resolve about the way to prepare for the Lord. Let us add that nothing ever happens where such yearning is absent. Second, you should have an example to learn from. Third, you must constantly and intently look to your Master, and see to it that you believe, obey, and follow Him. Fourth, you should set about the work and practice it. If one of these four breaks down, the art will never be learned and mastered.(42)

IV. Conclusion

In sum, we can find the following elements of a pagan, Germanic *Weltanschauung* in the *Theologia Germanica*:

1. God is presented as "worldly," rather than as a transcendent being. God is either in things, or things are in God, depending upon how you look at it.
2. The world is affirmed as good, as a paradise even. The negative is incorporated within the whole, rather than sundered from it.
3. Man and God are intimately involved with each other. Men can be divinized through allowing the divine spirit to come to be within them, and God requires the human soul to truly come to be in the world.
4. Coming to an awareness of eternal, divine truth is presented through the Odinic image of the sacrifice of one eye so that another may be opened.
5. The text develops at length an aristocratic, "warrior" ethics of detachment and disinterested performance of duty. Those who perform their duty for the wrong reasons are dismissed as "hirelings."
6. When the text discusses specific moral virtues, these again seem to stem from an aristocratic, chivalric standpoint.

If the tradition of Christian, German mysticism represents a continuation of a pre-Christian Germanic worldview, then this leads to a very exciting conclusion: the works of the German mystics—as well as those of the German philosophers they influenced, down to the modern period—could be regarded as laying bare the inner, mystical meaning of Germanic folk religion. Germanic religion has its Vedas: the *Eddas* and Sagas. But its Upanishads were never written. Can we regard the works of mystics like Hildegard von Bingen, Eckhart, Tauler, Cusa, Paracelsus, and others, as well as the philosophers influenced by them (chiefly Schelling, Hegel, and Heidegger) as providing, quite without intention, the equivalent of a Germanic Vedanta? The "Christian" character of German mysticism has been a deterrent to many who have sought an understanding of pre-Christian, Germanic thought. But if one regards the Christian character of German mysticism as in large measure a veneer, then these texts can be approached in an entirely new and exciting way.

Needless to say, my conclusions about what is Germanic in the *Theologia Germanica* (and in German mysticism in general) are open to objections stemming from disagreements as to what is and is not pagan and Germanic. Take point #1, for example. One might object that I seem to be saying that Germanic paganism was pantheistic. I am not saying that, however. I am merely saying that in Germanic myth the Gods are within the world, and involved with the world.(43) The world itself was created from the body of the titanic god Ymir. Needless to say, we do not find the same doctrine in the *Theologia Germanica*, but we do find, as in most of the German mystics, a tendency to want to bring the Christian God into the world, and most especially to involve him "organically" with the human individual.

Of course, there is much else that is "Germanic" in the *Theologia Germanica*. One can find what appear to be anticipations of positions held by later German thinkers. There are at least a couple of explanations for this. For example, it is remarkable how "Kantian" the ethical teaching of the *Theologia Germanica* is. This could simply be because through Luther, the ethics of the *Theologia Germanica* influenced German culture, including the German pietism in which Kant was raised as a boy. I think this explanation is entirely correct, however I also think that the ethics of the *Theologia Germanica* is, in a way, nothing new, but the expression of a certain perennial aspect of the German character. There are also statements in the *Theologia Germanica* which seem strikingly Hegelian and Heideggerean, yet there is no evidence that I know of that Hegel and Heidegger ever encountered the *Theologia Germanica*. There is a simple historical explanation for this, however. These same ideas and tendencies are present in thinkers that did exercise an influence on Hegel and Heidegger: notably Eckhart. Here again, however, I would agree and yet maintain at the same time that very often certain thinkers respond to certain ideas because those ideas have, for lack of a better word, a special kinship with them.

What we have in the *Theologia Germanica* is not only a document that exercised a direct and indirect historical influence on others, but also the expression of a *philosophia Germanica perennis*.(44) And isn't this what Luther saw when he titled this untitled text simply "A German Theology"?

Notes

(1) *The Theologia Germanica of Martin Luther*, trans. Bengt Hoffman (Mahwah, New Jersey: The Paulist Press, 1980), 54. All quotations from the work will come from Hoffman's translation, which will be referred to in the notes as *Theologia Germanica*. Editions of the *Theologia Germanica*, including German editions, are maddeningly inconsistent in how they divide and number the chapters of the work, and whether they follow the original, shorter version of the text, or the Würzburg manuscript, or some combination. I have employed the following German edition of the *Theologia Germanica*: *Der Frankfurter: Eine Deutsche Theologie*, ed. Joseph Berhhart (Leipzig, 1922). This is an edition of the Würzburg manuscript. In some cases, I have altered Hoffman's translation, and where I thought a particular word or phrase to be especially significant, I have included the original German.

(2) In my discussion of the history of the *Theologia Germanica*, as well as the cultural context surrounding it, I am relying in the main on Bengt Hoffman's excellent introduction to his translation.

(3) Lewis White Beck, *Early German Philosophy* (Cambridge, Mass: Harvard University Press, 1969), 41.

(4) James Russell, *The Germanization of Early Medieval Christianity: A Sociohistorical Approach to Religious Transformation* (New York: Oxford University Press, 1994).

(5) Russell, 39.

(6) Ibid., 102.

(7) Ibid., 23.

(8) Ibid., 40.

(9) A point made by Russell, ibid., 39.

(10) See Julius Evola, *The Doctrine of Awakening: The Attainment of Self-Mastery According to the Earliest Buddhist Texts*, trans. H.E. Musson (Rochester, Vermont: Inner Traditions, 1996).

(11) Other authors have discerned the striking "Germanness" of the *Theologia Germanica*. The Englishman Christian Bunsen, whose enthusiasm for the *Theologia Germanica* led to its being translated into English in 1874, said that our text was "the first protest of the Germanic mind against the Judaism and formalism of the Byzantine and medieval churches, the hollowness to which their scholasticism had led, and the rottenness of society which a pompous hierarchy strove in vain to conceal, but had not the power nor the will to correct." Quoted in Bengt Hoffman p. 32.

(12) *Theologia Germanica*, 60.

(13) *Theologia Germanica*, 60.

(14) *Theologia Germanica*, Chapter Sixteen, 82.

(15) *Theologia Germanica*, Chapter Thirty-Four, 108. It should be noted that while in this passage, and others, the *Theologia Germanica* sounds strikingly Heideggerean, the author is inconsistent in treating God both as *a* being (albeit the most exalted) and as the Being *of* beings.

(16) *Theologia Germanica*, Chapter Twenty, 86.
(17) *Theologia Germanica*, Chapter Forty-Five, 134.
(18) *Theologia Germanica*, Chapter Fifty-Five, 148.
(19) *Theologia Germanica*, Chapter Forty-Seven, 136.
(20) *Theologia Germanica*, 60.
(21) *Theologia Germanica*, Chapter One, 61.
(22) *Theologia Germanica*, Chapter Two, 61.
(23) *Theologia Germanica*, Chapter Three, 62.
(24) Ibid., 63.

(25) This point is discussed extensively in Stephen E. Flowers, *The Northern Dawn*, Vol. 1 (Smithville, Texas: Runa-Raven Press, 2006), 24-26.

(26) *Theologia Germanica*, Chapter Fourteen, 80.

(27) *Theologia Germanica*, Chapter Seven, 67. Eckhart speaks of an "outer" and "inner man," and this may be the inspiration for our author's distinction between an "outer" and "inner" eye.

(28) Ibid., 68.
(29) *Theologia Germanica*, 165, translator's note 37.
(30) *Theologia Germanica*, Chapter Seventeen, 83.
(31) *Theologia Germanica*, Chapter Twenty-One, 88.
(32) Ibid., 88.
(33) *Theologia Germanica*, Chapter Thirty-Three, 107.
(34) *Theologia Germanica*, Chapter Five, 64.
(35) *Theologia Germanica*, Chapter Sixteen, 82.
(36) *Theologia Germanica*, Chapter Twenty-Four, 93. Italics added.
(37) *Theologia Germanica*, Chapter Ten, 71.
(38) *Theologia Germanica*, Chapter Thirty-Seven, 114.
(39) *Theologia Germanica*, Chapter Thirty, 103-104.
(40) *Theologia Germanica*, Chapter Thirty-Six, 111.
(41) *Theologia Germanica*, Chapter Twenty-Five, 97.
(42) *Theologia Germanica*, Chapter Twenty, 87.

(43) Nevertheless, I shall quote Heinrich Heine: "No one says it, but everyone knows it: pantheism is the open secret of Germany. We have, in fact, outgrown deism. . . . Deism is a religion for slaves, for children, for Genevese, for watchmakers. Pantheism is the occult religion of Germany, and this result was foreseen by those German writers who, fifty years ago, let loose their zealotry against Spinoza." Heinrich Heine, *Religion and Philosophy in Germany*, trans. John Snodgrass (Albany: State University of New York Press, 1986), 79. Of Schelling, Heine writes, "He restored that great philosophy of nature

which, after unobtrusively budding out of the old pantheistic religion of the Germans, displayed during the age of Paracelsus its fairest flowers, but was stifled by the introduction of Cartesianism." Ibid., 155.

(44) This is how J.N. Findlay describes Hegel's philosophy in his *Hegel: A Re-Examination* (New York: Oxford University Press, 1958), 49.

The State of Traditional Germanic and Scandinavian Studies in the Universities of the United States

Michael Moynihan

One of the primary goals of the Woodharrow Institute is the preservation and promotion of traditional academic study concerning ancient Germanic culture, as well as the more archaic Indo-European origins from which that culture arose. The history of serious scholarly work dealing with the early Germanic world goes back several centuries. As with any discipline, influences from intellectual fads have affected Germanic Studies in varying ways over the course of time, and there have likewise been periods of great breakthroughs in knowledge and understanding. The eighteenth and nineteenth centuries witnessed unfolding discoveries about the common Indo-European roots of various languages and cultures, and in the early decades of the 1800s the field of Germanic Studies received great impetus from the pioneering work of Jacob Grimm and his brother Wilhelm. Their works remain important sources for the discipline to the present day.

By the early decades of the twentieth century an impressive amount of reliable knowledge had accumulated, and traditional Germanic Studies entered into a particularly fruitful phase. It would only be in the wake of the Second World War that negative sentiments concerning Germany seriously began to impact this vibrant scholarly field. Yet even twenty to thirty years ago, large and multifaceted departments with a focus on traditional Germanic culture and language were still thriving at a considerable number of U.S. universities. The same was true of the related discipline of Scandinavian Studies, as is evident from an article, circa June 1971, by Gene G. Gage published in the *Bibliography of Old Norse and Icelandic Studies (BONIS)*.(1) Entitled "The Teaching of Old Norse–Icelandic in the United States," the article compiles data on the number of academic institutions in this country offering courses in the Old Norse and Icelandic languages and their cultural-historical background. The second paragraph (p.7) is illustrative of the findings at that time:

> The fact that courses in Old Norse, Old and Modern Icelandic, Medieval Scandinavian Literature, and Nordic Mythology were taught at thirty institutions in the U.S. is an impressive figure in itself. When one

considers that at least 44 scholars were involved in the teaching of nearly 70 courses during just one academic year, it is apparent that faculties, deans, and departmental chairmen are recognizing the value of, and need for, courses in Old Norse. And, with more than 400 students enrolled in 30 courses during the fall semester/quarter alone, it can be stated, without fear of contradiction, that Old Norse-Icelandic Studies in America have reached their highest level in history.

Following some discussion on the methods of data collection used to gather this information, a detailed list of the thirty institutions offering these courses was provided at the end of the article.

Times have clearly changed. While the situation may have looked bright in 1971, over the last three decades nearly *half* of these schools have ceased teaching in these areas. The general situation concerning traditional Germanic academic programs has also unquestionably worsened, particularly since the 1980s. Many programs are pale reflections of their previous incarnations, or have forsaken pre-1500 Germanic Studies altogether and instead focus solely on modern languages, literature, and especially culture.

The present article makes no attempt to seriously analyze the whys and wherefores of this decline, which are undoubtedly complex and based on a confluence of factors. The liberal arts curriculum—of which Germanic Studies have always been a part—has suffered in general as American culture continues to place greater emphasis on business and technology. So while Germanic Studies programs have been increasingly neglected by university administrations over the past thirty years, the same is probably true of other liberal arts subjects such as Classical Studies or Philosophy—higher degrees in these areas do not have great "market value." The reality of limited job opportunities has provided an economic rationale for administrations to pare away at programs, with traditional areas of study sometimes being hit the hardest. In the prevailing world of modernity and globalization, where all emphasis is placed on the future, the study of the ancient European languages and cultures of the "deep past" may seem quaintly irrelevant. And as elements of the traditional Western canon, these subjects may also be considered in some quarters as politically incorrect, reactionary holdovers.

Despite the above-mentioned setbacks, there are still a number of fine traditional Germanic Studies programs in existence in the U.S., led by very able scholars and teachers. The present article aims to provide a listing of these, along with some details on course offerings and specific instructors. This survey does not claim to be exhaustive; it is quite possible that some programs, or the remnants thereof, which still offer valuable opportunities in this area may have been inadvertently overlooked.(2) The information contained here was accurate at the time of writing (fall, 2006). Interested students will need to check directly with the programs in question to determine their current faculty and course offerings.

The main programs listed have been included because they have at least one specialist in early Germanic or Scandinavian cultures and languages, offer courses in multiple Germanic languages, and have M.A. or Ph.D. programs in which a student can focus on traditional topics. Many institutions with good postgraduate offerings will also have undergraduate programs that encourage study in these areas. In the latter part of the article I will also provide a selective list of some noted professors whose expertise would be of great benefit to an enthusiastic student of early Germanic culture, even if the institutions where they teach do not currently provide a larger program that supports this particular area of study. A reference list of Internet webpage addresses for all the programs referred to appears at the end of the article.

There are a number of programs available on the West Coast. The most comprehensive of these seems to be at the University of California at Los Angeles. Here the Department of Germanic Studies offers M.A. and Ph.D. programs with the option for an Old Norse Studies track. Numerous courses in Old Norse language, literature, and culture are presently being taught, many of them by the noted author and translator Jesse Byock (author of *Viking Age Iceland* [2001] and translator of *The Saga of the Volsungs* [1990]). In the 1970s UCLA developed an innovative and respected Indo-European Studies program that still exists to this day. This Ph.D. program is based upon cross-listed courses from various departments. Represented among these are historical Indo-European languages such as the older Germanic (Gothic, Old High German, Old Saxon, Old English), Indic, and Iranian; Baltic and Slavic folklore and mythology; Celtic languages and mythology; and so forth.

The German Department at the University of California at Berkeley has M.A. and Ph.D. programs in German literature and culture, or Germanic linguistics. The latter track specifically features courses in Old High German, Old Saxon, Gothic and relevant subjects taught by Irmengard Rauch. The Scandinavian department has M.A. and Ph.D. graduate programs. Carol Clover (author of *The Medieval Saga* [1982]) and John Lindow (author of a number of books and reference works concerning Norse mythology) teach courses in Old Norse language and literature, early Scandinavian history and culture, and medieval Scandinavian history and culture. Many of these courses specifically relate to myth and religion.

Stanford University offers M.A. and Ph.D. programs through its Department of German. Orrin W. Robinson teaches Gothic, Old High German, Middle High German, and a course on the fairytales of the Brothers Grimm. There is also an interdepartmental undergraduate program in Medieval Studies.

In the Pacific Northwest, the University of Washington at Seattle has a long-standing and strong tradition of Scandinavian Studies. Patricia Conroy teaches courses in Old Icelandic and Old Norse, saga literature, Northern European ballads, and the history of the Scandinavian languages. Much of the department is devoted to modern language instruction, which is very comprehensive. More recently a Baltic Studies program—focused on language, history, and culture—has also developed under the auspices of the department. The Department of Germanics has two professors who both teach in areas of Indo-European and Germanic historical linguistics, Charles Barrack and Joseph Voyles (who is also an adjunct professor in the linguistics dept.).

In the Midwest, the Department of Germanic Languages and Literatures at the University of Kansas at Lawrence offers M.A. and Ph.D. programs. An undergraduate course is also offered in Germanic mythology, religion, and folklore. In the Linguistics department, Donald Watkins teaches courses in Germanic linguistics, including an introductory course in Old Norse.

The University of Nebraska at Lincoln's Department of Modern Languages offers M.A. and Ph.D. programs in German, with a concentration on medieval literature or philology. With the recent retirement of Dieter Karch, however, courses in older Germanic languages such as Gothic and Old High German are no longer being offered regularly.

The University of Minnesota is well known for its support of Scandinavian Studies. The Department of German, Scandinavian, and Dutch offers M.A. and Ph.D. programs in which a Germanic Medieval Studies track is an option. An M.A. focused in Scandinavian Studies is also available. Kaaren Grimstad and Anatoly Liberman teach courses in Old Norse, Old Icelandic, Gothic, Old Saxon, Old High German, Middle High German, heroic literature, Scandinavian mythology, saga and Eddic literature, and German folklore. Evelyn Firchow teaches in the areas of Germanic philology and medieval German literature. Ray Wakefield also teaches courses in Germanic Medieval Studies. The department annually offers a six-week course in modern Icelandic.

The University of Wisconsin at Madison maintains its traditionally strong German department, offering M.A. and Ph.D. programs. A track is available concentrating on literature and culture before 1600, including Middle High German and older Germanic languages. The university's Department of Scandinavian Studies has M.A. and Ph.D. programs concentrated on literature or philology. Thomas Dubois (author of *Nordic Religions in the Viking Age* [1999]) and Kirsten Wolf teach courses in Old Norse, Old Norse paleography and philology, mythology of Scandinavia, Icelandic sagas, Finnish, and Scandinavian linguistics.

Indiana University at Bloomington has a Germanic Studies department with M.A. and Ph.D. programs concentrating on older Germanic and Scandinavian language and culture. Kari Ellen Gade (author of *The Structure of Old Norse Dróttkvætt Poetry* [1995]) teaches courses in Old Norse language and literature, runes and runic inscriptions, Viking culture and sagas, as well as older Germanic languages including Gothic, Old Saxon, Old High German, and Middle High German.

In Ann Arbor the University of Michigan's Germanic Languages and Literatures department offers M.A. and Ph.D. programs with a joint degree in Germanic languages and linguistics. Courses in Old Norse, Gothic, and Middle High German have been offered. More importantly, the department offers a modest undergraduate program in the area of Scandinavian Studies. Astrid Beck teaches the courses relating to Old Norse mythology and literature. Teaching at the University of Michigan Law School is also William Ian Miller (author of *Bloodtaking and Peacemaking: Feud, Law, and Society in Saga Iceland* [1990] and *Law and Literature in Medieval Iceland* [with Theodore Andersson, 1989], who has active interests in the areas of Medieval Studies and the Icelandic sagas.

The University of Illinois at Urbana-Champaign has a very strong Department of Germanic Languages and Literatures offering M.A. and Ph.D. programs concentrated on older German literature, Germanic linguistics, or Scandinavian. Frederick Schwink (a former student of Edgar Polomé and Winfred Lehmann at the University of Texas) teaches in the areas of Germanic and Indo-European linguistics. Courses are offered in Old Norse, Old High German, and other older Germanic languages. Claudia Bornholdt and Stephen Jaeger teach courses relating to Germanic and Scandinavian Medieval Studies, including Viking mythology and German folklore. The Department of Linguistics also offers a Ph.D. program with an optional area concentration on Germanic.

In the Southwest, the Department of Germanic Studies at the University of Texas at Austin has one of the largest German programs in the country. Both M.A. and Ph.D. programs are available, and in the latter program a primary area of concentration can be directed toward Germanic linguistics and philology, medieval German literature, or Scandinavian languages and literature. John Weinstock teaches courses in Old Norse language, Viking culture and religion, and Sámi culture. A survey course in older Germanic languages is offered. UT-Austin is also the home of the A. Richard Diebold Center for Indo-European Language and Culture, established by Brigitte Bauer and Carol Justus. Dr. Justus, of the Classics department, also teaches a course specifically in the area of Indo-European language and culture. The university further offers an interdisciplinary Medieval Studies graduate program.

The University of New Mexico offers an interdepartmental Medieval Studies program through its English department, granting the M.A. and Ph.D. The program includes courses taught by Helen Damico in Old English, Old Norse, Viking culture, and *Beowulf*. Other courses cover topics such as Iron Age Europe, Viking mythology, and early Celtic cultures. The university is also home to the Institute for Medieval Studies which in past years has hosted lecture series on themes such as "Medieval Scandinavian Culture," "The Celts," and "Barbarian Europe."

On the East Coast, the University of North Carolina at Chapel Hill offers M.A. and Ph.D. programs in German literature through its Department of Germanic Languages. Kathryn Starkey teaches in areas of Old Norse, Gothic, Old High German, Old Saxon, paleography, saga literature, Viking age culture, and medieval "ritual and representation."

The University of Maryland at College Park offers M.A. and Ph.D. programs through their Department of Germanic Studies, with a possible concentration on older languages and literature. Rose-Marie Oster teaches a course in ancient Germanic religion, and courses are offered in Old Norse, Gothic, Old High German and Middle High German, as well as Germanic mythology. The program description also refers to seminars being offered in Germanic or Indo-European philology that deal with runology and Eddic and skaldic poetry. It is, however, very possible that these particular offerings might no longer be available with the recent retirement of the Indo-Europeanist and Scandinavianist Jere Fleck from the department.

The University of Connecticut offers an M.A. and Ph.D. program in Medieval Studies. The program is co-directed by Robert Hasenfratz, whose personal expertise lies in the areas of Old Norse, Old English, *Beowulf*, and Middle English. Frederick Biggs teaches Old English, Middle English, and Old Irish language and literature. The university is also home to the recently established New England Saga Society, which hosts and sponsors sessions at academic conferences.

Harvard University's Department of Germanic Languages and Literatures offers M.A. and Ph.D. programs with a possible concentration on pre-1500 older languages and literatures. Stephen Mitchell teaches courses in Old Norse language and literature, mythology, Viking culture, and related topics. Joseph Harris in the English department teaches Old Norse and Old English and related topics. Jay Jasanoff, Professor of Indo-European Linguistics and Philology, teaches courses in the history of Indo-European languages. The Department of Celtic Languages and Literatures is notably strong at Harvard, and includes Patrick K. Ford (translator of *The Mabinogi* [1977]). There is also an interdepartmental undergraduate program in Myth and Folklore.

The University of Massachusetts at Amherst offers an M.A. and Ph.D. program through its Department of German and Scandinavian Studies, with concentrations available in medieval literature and Germanic philology. James E. Cathey (editor of *Hêliand: Text and Commentary*, 2002) and Robert G. Sullivan teach courses in Old Norse, Gothic, Old Saxon, Old High German, Middle High German, and medieval literature. Sherrill Harbison teaches courses in Scandinavian mythology, saga literature, Nordic romanticism, and related topics. In the English department Stephen J. Harris teaches courses in Old English, *Beowulf*, history of the English language, and medieval literature; a course in Old Irish is also offered through the Comparative Literature department. Courses relevant to Indo-European historical linguistics are available through the Classics department.

Cornell University offers M.A. and Ph.D. programs through its German Studies department, with a minor concentration available in Old Norse, as well as a concentration in older Germanic languages. As part of the Medieval Studies program, Oren Falk of the History department teaches in areas of Old Norse language, epic, and medieval Scandinavian culture. Cornell's library is home to the Fiske Icelandic Collection, a major resource for Icelandic history and literature, as well as a large witchcraft collection.

Yale University's Department of English offers courses in *Beowulf*, Old Norse, Old Norse poetry and prose, and medieval topics taught by Roberta Frank. The Department of Linguistics offers M.A. and Ph.D. programs with a concentration on Indo-European. Stanley Isler teaches many of these courses, including a comparative study of older Germanic languages.

In addition to the aforementioned university programs with offerings in older Germanic languages and culture, it is also worth noting some specific instructors at other institutions whose areas of expertise and research fall along these lines.

Craig R. Davis is Professor of English at Smith College (a private women's liberal arts school) in Northampton, Massachusetts. He teaches courses in Old and Middle English, *Beowulf*, Old Norse, and Medieval Welsh. He is the author of *'Beowulf' and the Demise of Germanic Legend in England* (1996).

Stephen O. Glosecki is an Associate Professor of English at the University of Alabama at Birmingham. He is the author of *Shamanism in Old English Poetry* (1989), and teaches courses in Old English, literature of the Vikings, and "images of the outlaw."

Michael J. Enright, the author of *Lady with a Mead Cup* (1996), teaches in the Department of History at East Carolina University at Greenville.

Edward R. Haymes is Professor of German and Comparative Literature at Cleveland State University. He is the author of *Heroic*

Legends of the North (with Susann Samples, 1996), and translator of *The Saga of Thidrek of Bern* (1988).

Paul Bauschatz teaches courses in Old English language and literature in the English department at the University of Maine at Orono. He is the author of *The Well and the Tree* (1982).

G. Ronald Murphy is Associate Professor of German at Georgetown University. He is the translator of *The Heliand* (1992) and author of *The Saxon Savior* (1989).

It is hoped the information provided here will be of use to prospective students wishing to pursue the study of ancient Germanic and Indo-European culture. In order for the schools to continue to make these educational opportunities available, they must be convinced there is a serious desire and need from a sector of the student body to study and engage with these disciplines, both now and in the long-term future. And as importantly, they must continue to recognize the essential role of traditional Germanic Studies in Western intellectual and academic culture, and the considerable relevance it bears to many other scholarly disciplines including Archeology, Comparative Religion, History, History of Religions, and Philosophy.

If university administrations remain idle in the face of present trends, however, the existing programs will continue to slowly erode. Retiring professors with expertise in this area will not be replaced; the result being that traditional Germanic Studies will ultimately die on the vine at these institutions. A comparison with the situation just a few decades ago shows how this has already occurred in all too many instances. This creates a vicious circle, for if existing programs lapse, career positions for future scholars and teachers of traditional Germanic Studies disappear. With a landscape of ever-diminishing job opportunities for those who pursue this field of study, the remaining programs will have less and less justification for support from their respective university administrations. Unless this negative momentum can somehow be countered and reversed, the prospects look grim. Needless to say, this general situation is one of the main reasons why the Woodharrow Institute has come into existence at the present point in time.

Notes

(1) The article appears in the 1970 volume of *BONIS* (*Bibliography of Old Norse-Icelandic Studies*), 7–21.

(2) The Woodharrow Institute would appreciate any information concerning relevant programs, opportunities, or individuals that have not been noted here, as well as updated information on the listed programs. The present article only concerns the United States; an article in a future issue of *Symbel* may examine the opportunities that exist in other parts of the world. This article also does not attempt to examine the offerings in English departments across the country, but it is likely that the better of these will contain at least one professor who specializes in Old English; these

professors may also offer occasional courses in Old Norse. Students interested specifically in Old English should investigate such opportunities. Useful information might also be gleaned from the International Society of Anglo-Saxonists (www.isas.us).

WWW Addresses for Programs & Schools Mentioned in This Article:
(URLs are for Germanic language departments unless otherwise noted)

University of California at Los Angeles: www.germanic.ucla.edu
UCLA Indo-European Studies: www.humnet.ucla.edu/pies/home.html
University of California at Berkeley: http://german.berkeley.edu
UC-Berkeley Scandinavian Studies: http://ls.berkeley.edu/dept/scandinavian
Stanford University: www.stanford.edu/dept/german
University of Washington, Scandinavian Studies: http://depts.washington.edu/scand
University of Washington, Baltic Studies: http://depts.washington.edu/baltic
University of Kansas: http://www2.ku.edu7germanic
University of Kansas, Linguistics: www.linguistics.ku.edu
University of Nebraska, Modern Languages: www.unl.edu/modlang/Index.html
University of Minnesota: www.gsd.umn.edu
University of Wisconsin at Madison: http://german.lss.wisc.edu
University of Wisconsin at Madison, Scandinavian Studies:
   http://scandinavian.wisc.edu
Indiana University: www.indiana.edu7germanic
University of Michigan: www.lsa.umich.edu/german/german
University of Illinois at Urbana-Champaign: www.germanic.uiuc.edu/
University of Illinois at Urbana-Champaign, Linguistics: www.linguistics.uiuc.edu
University of Texas at Austin: www.utexas.edu/depts/german/main.html
A. Richard Diebold Center for Indo-European Languages:
   www.utexas.edu/cola/depts/lrc/ARD.html
UT-Austin, Medieval Studies: www.utexas.edu/cola/progs/medievalstudies/
University of New Mexico, Medieval Studies:
   www.unm.edu/%7eenglish/MedievalStudies/index.htm
University of New Mexico Institute for Medieval Studies: www.unm.edu7medinst/
University of North Carolina: www.unc.edu/depts/german
University of Maryland: www.languages.umd.edu/German
University of Connecticut, Medieval Studies: http://medievalstudies.uconn.edu/
New England Saga Society: www.medievalstudies.uconn.edu/ness.htm
Harvard University: www.fas.harvard.edu7german
University of Massachusetts at Amherst: www.umass.edu/germanic
Cornell University: www.arts.cornell.edu/german/index.html
Cornell University, Medieval Studies: www.arts.cornell.edu/medieval
Yale University, Department of English: www.yale.edu/english
Yale University, Linguistics: www.yale.edu/linguist
Smith College, Deptartment of English: www.smith.edu/english
University of Alabama at Birmingham: www.uab.edu
East Carolina University at Greenville: www.ecu.edu
Cleveland State University: www.csuohio.edu
University of Maine at Orono: www.umaine.edu
Georgetown University: www.georgetown.edu

Reviews

Brian Murdoch and Malcolm Read, eds. *Early Germanic Literature and Culture*. The Camden House History of German Literature Volume 1. Rochester/Woodbridge: Camden House, 2004. x + 334 pp. www.camden-house.com

This is a volume which has been much needed for quite some time. The student of early Germanic culture is often hampered initially by a severe dearth of high quality recent scholarship which is directed in a more general and broad way to those who are not already experts in various fields of Germanic philology and cultural studies. In this task *Early Germanic Literature and Culture* succeeds admirably.

The book is the first volume in a ten volume series on the history of German literature. However, as a reasonable inauguration of such an undertaking this initial volume takes on the problems of a more general and holistic cultural and historical nature. This survey consists of a useful introduction followed by eleven substantial essays on various topics in early Germanic literature, language, culture and religion—all by leading scholars in the relevant fields, e.g. Heinrich Beck on "The Concept of Germanic Antiquity," Herwig Wolfram on "*Origo gentis*: The Literature of German Origins," Rudolf Simek on "Germanic Religion and the Conversion to Christianity," Klaus Düwel on "Runic," Theodor Anderson on "Old Norse-Icelandic Literature," Fred C. Robinson on "Old English," and G. Ronald Murphy on "The Old Saxon *Heliand*."

As a possible textbook for an introductory course in early Germanic culture, this book would prove a valuable teaching tool.

Stephen E. Flowers

John McKinnell and Rudolf Simek with Klaus Düwel. *Runes, Magic and Religion: A Sourcebook*. Studia Medievalia Septentrionalia 10. Vienna: Fassbinder, 2004. 224 pp. www.fassbaender.com

In the world of present-day academic runology no one topic stirs more passion than that of "magic." At the beginning of the scientific study of runes—going all the way back to Johannes Bureus—few if any ever doubted the magical or religious significance of the runes to at least some of the ancient Germanic peoples. This is most probably because almost every medieval reference to the runes endowed them with this aura of mystcal awe, and the inscriptions themselves often self-referentially indicate that the runes possess a special quality or nature which separates them from the ordinary, mundane world. They might be called "descended from the gods" (**raginaku(n)do** on the sixth-century Noleby stone) or referred to as "eternal" (e.g. the *ævinrúnaR* on the ninth-century Malt stone). In the literature the myth of their "discovery" by the god Óðinn is conspicuous ("Hávamál" 138-164). The word *rún* is so often compounded with other linguistic elements which indicate some operative, mystical or magical function that every early observer merely took it for granted that the *rūnōz* → *rúnar*: "mysteries" had to have something to do with the sphere or human activity usually referred to in modern terms as "religious" or "magical." This early trend was, however, somewhat misguided as the assumptions usually tended to liberate the scholar from establishing the discussion of runes and magic in any current scientific theoretical context. (This is what I attempted to do with my dissertation and subsequent book, *Runes and Magic*.) To study the topic of runes and magic scientifically we should, most logically, take into account: 1) runology (as a subset of early Germanic philology) and 2) cultural anthropology (ethnology) or folklore (the fields in which the topic of magic is studied academically).

McKinnell does not attempt to address the fields of magic or religion in any scientific manner. Readers are left, as they are with most current books approaching this subject, to supply their own ready-made, subjective and usually unscientific estimations of what *magic* or even *religion* are. If those who study admittedly obscure and difficult data such as those represented by runes, and other inscriptions of various cultural origins, would first make themselves familiar with the auxiliary scientific disciplines necessary for a comprehensive interpretation of those data then further *advancement* might be made in the field of runology. As it stands now the "magical" *versus* "non-magical" schools of interpretation appear to ride on a pendulum of academic fashion. If magic is "in" there is no need to establish a theoretical basis for what is obviously "true," and by the same token if magic is "out of fashion" as an interpretation equally no need is felt to support this opinion in any comprehensive or scientific way.

An example of how the application of current scientific theory on magic has made progress in a parallel field is provided by the work of Prof. Dr. John Gager, whose book *Curse Tablets and Binding Spells from the Ancient World* (Oxford, 1992), focuses a similar theoretical framework as that used in *Runes and Magic* on a corpus of inscriptions from Mediterranean culture.

Obviously the strength of *Runes, Magic and Religion* does not lie in its theoretical foundation nor in its general analysis of the runic tradition, rather it resides in the useful categorization of types of inscriptions and the individual discussions of the inscriptions within these categories. Its chief usefulness lies in its broad catalog of runic inscriptions from all cultural spheres and time periods (early Germanic, Old English, Frisian, German and Norse). Although this catalog does not pretend to be complete, it is a sizable sample of the most important inscriptions with possible magical or religious implications. Significantly, the work shows how much of the magical reputation of the runes was carried over from traditional practice into Christian times.

Stephen E. Flowers

Greg Mogenson. *Northern Gnosis: Thor, Baldr, and the Volsungs in the Thought of Freud and Jung*.New Orleans: Spring Journal Books, 2005. xx + 140 pp. www.springjournalandbooks.com

In these times it is a rare pleasure to see the mythic paradigms of Germania utilized in the context of a thoughtful discussion of current philosophical or psychological issues. It has long been a contention of mine that certain keys to psychological problems could be gained by discovering the way our own ancestors thought about various aspects— concrete and subtle—which make up the whole human being. As the ancient Germanic peoples (as well as other Indo-Europeans) had a dozen terms relating to these anthropological faculties— the *lík*: "body," *hugr*: "mind," *minni*: "memory," *hamr*: "shape," *fylgja*: "accompanying spirit," etc., it stands to reason that these ancients were in some way or another intimately familiar with a variety of subtle variations in spiritual experience which has been more or less lost to us. Over the past century modern psychology has, in usually cumbersome ways, attempted to recover this previously familiar inner terrain.

Mogenson's book is not an attempt to do this. Rather it is an illumination of the ideas and writings of the two most important psychologists of the early 20th century—Sigmund Freud and Carl Gustav Jung—with images from Norse myth. The author sees modern psychology as a "new mythologem" which is both heir to an ancient tradition and something which supersedes or overthrows that tradition. this tension between the urge to continue what is good and venerable and to create something new, and (it is hoped) better, is inherent in the works of modern psychology. Mogenson says (p. 130) "Self-realization, according to Jung, is both the recognition of one's rootedness in the ancestral soul and an ahistorical break with tradition." Furthermore Jung states "... inauguration is the prerogative of man." (*Collected Works* vol. 10 § 268). In this we are reminded of the cosmogony in Eddic literature where the god Óðinn, himself the product of an evolutionary process organized from basic elements, is possessed of consciousness and rebels against the established order in an effort to create a more perfect cosmos.

This book does presuppose some basic familiarity with the intellectual worlds of Freud and Jung. The work would have been improved with some discussion of the existence of the archaic, traditional psychology possessed by the ancient Germanic peoples, which is only dimly approximated by modern psychologists. We await the appearance of Ingrid Fischer's work on this topic.

Mogenson's work tries to liberate psychological mythologizing from the tyranny of the South with its constant references to Greek myth to begin to show the degree to which Northern paradigms might indeed be present in the ideas of Freud and Jung. As one of Jung's intellectual heirs, James Hillman, "re-visioned" psychology from the perspective of Greek polytheism, Mogenson seems to suggest to us to look to Germanic religion for a similar "re-visioning." He is to be applauded for this stimulating exercise in the use of Germanic myth to articulate actual and present human problems.

Stephen E. Flowers

Stephen E. Flowers. *The Northern Dawn,* Volume 1. Smithville, Texas: Rûna-Raven, 2005. xvi + 144 pp. www.runaraven.com

This book represents the first part of a projected three-volume work, as well as a fresh perspective on Western history that should be welcomed by scholar and layman alike. What Dr. Flowers has attempted with *The Northern Dawn* seems to be unprecedented, for I know of no equivalent elsewhere. The "dawn" of the title is nothing less the conscious recognition and reestablishment of our Germanic cultural heritage. As this book proves, and although many people may not realize or comprehend it, such a reawakening (to use Flowers's preferred terminology) is part of an ongoing historical phenomenon.

In the introductory chapter entitled "Ways of Understanding," Flowers explains: "Perhaps the greatest misunderstanding which blocks the northern light is the idea that the old traditions were 'lost' when the Germanic peoples 'converted' to Christianity and that what was lost can never be found again."(p. 1) One primary aim of the book is to counteract these notions. He then defines the key concepts of his study: "Germanic," "culture," "religious transformation" (i.e., "conversion"), and "reawakening." He believes—and makes a very strong case for the idea—that Germanic cultural values were not extirpated during the conversion process, but merely submerged and repressed into a state of dormancy. Over the past millennium these values have occasionally reasserted themselves, although this has generally occurred in a piecemeal and limited fashion. Given the right circumstances, however, they could be fully "reawakened" and allowed to bloom once again. In his view, the favorable circumstances consist of these critical elements: a conscious desire for the reawakening, an array of sound and truthful sources for the cultural values in question, and a methodology for understanding both the sources and the historical background of the reawakening process. *The Northern Dawn* addresses all these elements, but is especially focussed toward the methodological issue.

After explaining his proposed methodology (which he notes could be similarly employed for any "nativistic culture"), Flowers spends subsequent chapters discussing the Germanic tradition in detail, the arrival of Christianity and the patterns of Christianization, the "Dark Ages" and later Medieval period, as well as the specific cultural-historical cases of the continental Germanic territories, England, Scandinavia, and Iceland.

Scholarship on archaic Germanic traditions and culture has always been strongest in Germany and Scandinavia, which is understandable. Here we have an English-language study of great breadth which analyzes these traditions, their sources, and their historical developments in a fascinating way. This first volume lays a solid groundwork for the inquiry, but it also becomes apparent that not until the beginning of the modern period will the necessary circumstantial elements for a Germanic reawakening really begin to fall into place. Since volume one ends with the late Medieval period, we are left looking forward to even more illuminating discoveries in the forthcoming installments of *The Northern Dawn*.

Michael Moynihan

Woodharrow Institute
for Germanic and Runic Studies

Goals

The present cultural environment has proven itself rather unsupportive of traditional knowledge and as each day goes by this lack of support seems to increase. Those who have an interest in the preservation, promotion and growth of education in the traditional cultural knowledge relating to the Germanic and Indo-European peoples now have a means to help remedy this kind of progressive cultural decay. It is the goal of the Woodharrow Institute to promote traditional fields of academic study relating to Germanic and Indo-European studies. It is our belief that the preservation of these studies where we find them, and their restoration where they have disappeared, will be of great benefit to society at large as we become increasingly aware of the deep cultural values from which we sprang. It is our ever increasing lack of awareness of our "culture of origin" that has led us to boredom within and conflict without. It is the goal of the Woodharrow Institute to provide access to academic and scientific research and methods to its general membership.

Projects
Educational Curriculum

Woodharrow implements its goals with a variety of effective means: First among these is the establishment of an educational curriculum in a full spectrum of traditional cultural studies, e.g. languages, literature, history, religious and mythic studies, and scientific runology. Woodharrow Institute courses are taught by individuals objectively qualified to teach at the college or university level. The Woodharrow Lore-House, or school, will specifically provide organized classes in the following fields: **Language** (German, modern Scandinavian dialects, [Old] Icelandic and Old English), **Cultural Studies** (Indo-European culture, history of religious ideas, Germanic culture in the Roman Age, Migration Age and Viking Age, Germanic myth and religion), **Literature** (history of Germanic literature before 1500, Old Norse poetry and prose, Old English poetry and prose, the *Eddas*, Romanticism and Neo-Romanticism), and **Runology** (older, younger and medieval, Anglo-Frisian and modern).

Today universities usually cost the student several thousand dollars per semester. It is the goal of Woodharrow to offer university-level instruction for a mere fraction of this cost. This is a historic opportunity.

Library / Archive

One of the main projects of Woodharrow is the development of a well-organized and sizable library collection of books, journals, off-prints, and other archival material relating to Germanic, Indo-European and runological studies. Libraries around the world have begun to neglect the collection of materials in these fields and so it becomes increasingly necessary for us to do it. It is hoped that a library facility can soon be erected and the collection moved to a location where it can be made available to the membership at large.

It has often been noted that the academic libraries around the world hold tremendous amounts of information that often prove extremely difficult to access for many who are interested in the material and who would greatly benefit from access to it. It is a goal of Woodharrow to collect such material and make it available to those who will be able to use it. The educational curriculum is the essential key to being able to use this material, as much of it will be in languages other than English.

The library is the laboratory of our school. Here we can learn of the ideas of scholars who have gone before us, and carry out a dialog with them. This library will become a permanent collection and will be passed on to future generations of members of the Woodharrow Institute. They will depend to a great extent on what we are able to collect and organize for them now. If we neglect this task, even more information will be lost in the future. Woodharrow accepts tax-deductible donations of books and other material for the library.

Lectures and Classes

The Institute also offers lectures and classes to the public at large on a wide variety of topics of general interest. Among these are: Our Mysterious Original Way of Writing: an Introduction to Runology, Our Ancient Tongue: the Beauty of Old English, Our Ancient Heritage and Destiny, Our Ancient Heritage and its Importance for Today. Members of the Woodharrow speakers' bureau can present these and other topics to the general public, clubs and associations, or to public and private schools.

Symbel

The official journal of the Woodharrow Institute is called *Symbel*. It acts as a forum for the presentation of the results of research in the fields of Germanic and runic studies, as well as other academic fields relating to Indo-European studies which might have played a part in the development of the Germanic cultural tradition. Articles which appear in *Symbel* will concentrate on themes relating to mythology, religion, and the history of ideas. A major feature of the journal will be translations of older scholarly articles from German and the Scandinavian dialects as well as reprints of older articles in English. *Symbel* will be available exclusively to members of Woodharrow.

Membership

What is needed at this time is for each and every person who feels it to be of vital personal importance to preserve and promote traditional knowledge and education in the ancient cultural values of the Germanic and Indo-European peoples to support the Woodharrow Institute. By becoming a member of Woodharrow you will be lending your tangible support to this worthy cause. Membership in the Woodharrow Institute is open to any and all individuals and families with an interest in the preservation and promotion of traditional cultural knowledge and values.

To become a member of the Woodharrow Institute write for more information to the addresses below, or consult our website for current information:

The Woodharrow Institute
seekthemysteries@gmail.com

To join and gain access to the Woodharrow talks, which are recorded presentations supplemented by PDFs, go to: www.woodharow.com. There is a large archive of material and new talks appear monthly. There is also a Facebook page: Woodharrow. Dr. Flowers can be reached directly at seekthemysteries@gmail.com.

www.ingramcontent.com/pod-product-compliance
Lightning Source LLC
Chambersburg PA
CBHW062119080426
42734CB00012B/2920